PARENTING TALENT

The Grown-Up's Guide
to Understanding and Supporting
Creatively Driven Teens and Tweens

DR. ALAINA JOHNSON

PARENTING TALENT

THE GROWN-UP'S GUIDE TO UNDERSTANDING AND SUPPORTING CREATIVELY DRIVEN TEENS AND TWEENS

DR. ALAINA JOHNSON

CONTENTS

To Alex, Zach, Gabe, and Kermit.
You make the journey a joyous one.
I love you.

Foreword

Darci Price, talent

manager

As a talent manager, I often joke that it wouldn't hurt if I had a degree in psychology. While my job isn't to be a therapist, this career does require me to play multiple roles, including adviser, cheerleader, confidant, coach, and friend. Each of our actors is wonderfully unique in who they are and the beauty they create. They are also special in terms of the varied techniques they employ to communicate and prepare their visions and bring them to life. One perfect approach does not exist. As a team, we learn what suits the client's style, and that often comes through trial and error. Because I love our clients and their parents, I have wished for a resource to help all of us better understand and expedite this process.

When Alaina shared that she was working on this book, selfishly, I couldn't have been more excited for her to complete it so that I could learn more ways to identify and support the needs of my young talent alongside their parents. The book is finally here! I now have an incredible resource to share with everyone. And guess what? This book is equally helpful for my adult clients! (Not to mention that I have learned a lot about myself—who knew?)

I have been a talent manager in Los Angeles since 2001, with a four-year detour into the talent agency world before returning to management. I represent actors and artists in the US and other countries. Their ages span from five to forty-five and counting. I work with a few clients in the newer stages of development, some who are "up-and-comers," and others who are "name talent." As part of my role, I help creatives find great opportunities, grow their careers, develop their skills, build stellar teams to achieve their dreams, and so much more on the business side. Other aspects of what I provide are guidance and resources to support the mental and emotional challenges inherent in a creative career. Like professional athletes, professionals in the arts require a strong mental outlook in addition to talent.

I first met Alaina in 2018, when two of her sons were referred to us by their prestigious New York talent agency. I knew they were established performers looking to amplify their existing forward momentum, but I wasn't familiar with their parents or how they approached the business.

Typically, a prospective client meeting lasts thirty to forty-five minutes, but our meeting easily hit two hours before we realized it. Within the first twenty minutes of our chat, though, I knew I loved the boys and that we wanted to work together—not only are they talented, but they also have the undeniable spark, joy, and drive that only come from loving one's art. I was certain that my management partner would see how special they were (and he does).

The balance of our meeting was spent socially because we had instantly bonded. Alaina is fun, joyful, interesting, and enlightened. She has a remarkable understanding of both the business and talent sides of the entertainment industry. Because of this, I was intrigued and asked if she had ever worked as a representative. It made sense when she told me that she is a therapist in addition to being the mother of three creative boys. She knows the reality, challenges, commitment, and expectations that come with a creative career, and she recognizes what her children need to navigate it all. In turn, her boys see the big picture because she and her husband have educated them in a way that they understand. This leads to healthier and more productive, creative kids.

Having worked with the Johnson family for several years now, I am constantly impressed with the growth and discovery the boys make with the support and guidance of their parents and the input of their creative team.

I continue to witness how Alaina's education and skill as a doctor, combined with her intuition and experience, elevate everyone around her. Add her pragmatic, critical-thinking mind and her nurturing spirit into the mix, and she qualifies as an expert.

Parenting Talent is exciting because no other resource helps a parent or mentor to easily identify the qualities and challenges of their creative tweens and teens, understand how they can best thrive, and take action to set their children up for success. This book is clearly laid out, supported by research, and illustrated with real-world examples. It is a game changer for artists and their families.

Preface

I didn't realize it at the time, but even before I had kids, I had a loosely formed picture in my mind of the type of parent I would be.

I knew that, as a psychologist, when I became a parent, I would read all of the latest and greatest—empirically validated, of course—parenting books and research I could find and implement accordingly.

My children would obviously enjoy school, and I would not have to remind them to complete their homework. Because I considered music education a valuable part of a well-rounded education, they would each be required to learn an instrument on a basic level—oh, and of course, they would all love to read during their downtime, as I do.

I would provide ample opportunities for a well-balanced mix of additional extracurricular activities—but not to the point of my children being overscheduled (the research supported ample free time).

I assumed team sports of some sort would be part of the journey for each of my kids. I was prepared to join the legions of parents I would see loading folding camping chairs, coolers, and gear bags into their trunks as uniformed kids scrambled into their cars. I would be a supportive, but never overbearing, sports mom, cheering my children on from the sidelines in the most appropriate manner.

Oh, I had a picture all right, and I assumed that with my many years as a babysitter, nanny, and camp counselor and my shiny new doctorate and internship at a children's hospital, even if the picture wasn't fully in focus, it certainly wasn't totally off the mark.

Perhaps you too have heard the phrase "never assume..."?

Unsurprisingly, soon after the birth of my first child, I quickly found that he had no knowledge of the fuzzy image in my head, and he was going to be exactly who he was, regardless of whether it matched up with my parenting fantasy. I soon found myself tossing out the books that didn't fit, gravitating toward the ones that did (whether they were empirically researched or not), and embracing whatever seemed to work best for our family.

This theme would not change and, in fact, would only grow stronger with the birth of my next two sons. Three boys, three very different personalities, who needed three different approaches to parenting. I did my best to adjust and understand and support them as individuals as much as I could.

In the beginning, one aspect of that image in my head did come into focus. As each boy reached the age of extracurriculars, we did, in fact, enroll them in a variety of activities in addition to piano lessons in order to explore what was a good fit.

My oldest was interested in and did well at multiple sports. He also expressed enjoyment of his piano lessons and other activities. He had an easygoing personality, and there was very little he wasn't open to trying at least once. My youngest added drum lessons to the required piano, and he rejected baseball for volleyball and football. While he was generally open to trying things out, if a particular activity wasn't his idea, he would demand a sound explanation for why he should engage in it.

My middle son was vocal from an early age that he was not particularly interested in team sports. When it came to baseball, he said, with six-year-old wisdom, "Why would I want to play a game where they throw a ball toward your head?"

He was the one who gave us our first hint of what was to come. By age two, he was singing nonstop, and at barely age three, he shocked my husband and me when we realized he could belt—in tune. By the time he was six, we were beginning to increasingly hear the word "talented" in connection to his singing voice and natural affinity for all things performance. We weren't sure what, if anything, to do with that feedback, so we soldiered on with his piano lessons and asked his instructor to add on some basic vocal training to help him avoid forming bad habits. Since we were team "well-rounded," when his classmates were signing up for soccer, we suggested he do so as well, and he agreed to try it as a compromise—since baseball had been so clearly dismissed from his options.

My husband and I raised our eyebrows at one another as he donned his uniform and I took the obligatory "my first game" photo of him. Yet he seemed happy enough as he took to the field with a few of his classmates on the same team. As we sat in the bleachers on the sidelines with the other parents, I joked, "My son is just as likely to be found picking daisies in the middle of an important play as running toward the ball." I was wrong. He did not pick daisies.

He ran and chased the ball until sweat was pouring down his face. At some point in the second period, he wiped sweat from his eyes and seemed to stop and think "Yep, enough. It's hot and I'm tired" and plunked down in the grass for an unsanctioned break. And... he proceeded to pick *dandelions*, which had taken over the grass field that day.

The photo I took of him sitting in the field still makes me laugh. Even though we weren't close enough to confirm, I would have bet good money that he was singing to himself as he watched the game continue on around him. That was the last team sport we signed him up for. Though he was athletic (and later earned a black belt in tae kwon do), he had no interest in the sports that many of his classmates would go on to play. He leaned in to what he loved: singing, dancing, acting, and his piano lessons.

As time went on, his peers began making last-minute plans on the baseball field after games where he was not present. I began to become concerned with making sure he had his own sense of community with friends who related to his passion for the arts. Though he seemed mostly content to explore his interests on his own, there were times when I could see he would have enjoyed exploring and discussing those interests with others who shared the same passions outside of his arts classes. As much as my husband and I supported his creative endeavors, we weren't always sure how to best help him navigate his artistry with constructive compassion.

I began searching for resources on how to positively support and encourage him while also helping him when he felt challenged or frustrated. When I looked for books on parenting kids who were into the creative arts, my search results would offer up multiple titles on how to encourage one's child's creativity. Not much came up about kids who were already creatively driven. Or I would find activities for children who were creative, but nothing about better understanding and supporting the way their creative minds worked. A search for "parenting talented children" inevitably brought up offerings on working with *intellectually* gifted and talented children, not *artistically* talented kids (not that kids can't be—and often are—both).

The few resources I was able to find that spoke to kids who were already invested in creative endeavors were largely focused on supporting child prodigies. We weren't trying to raise prodigies. I would have been happy if I could get my kids to remember to put their dishes in the dishwasher (note: still failing on that count). I just wanted some general guidance and validation that I was being as affirming as I could be.

After a while, I stopped looking and just got down to the business of trying to understand and navigate as best I could between my intuition, my parenting network, and my background in child and adolescent psychology. I also found myself bouncing my thoughts off fellow parents of creative kids.

During this time, our middle son had convinced us, after years of begging, to allow him to pursue representation by a local talent agency. I am not exaggerating—he was three when he first asked us if he could get an agent. We laughed and said, "I don't think you know what that is." He said, "Yes, I do. It's someone who can get people on TV, right?." After we picked our jaws up off of the ground, we offered a resounding no. He never stopped asking though, and four years later, we finally relented.

He was now enjoying participation in professional regional theater and occasional commercial bookings. Our youngest would occasionally have to accompany us to his agent's office for auditions, and he, too, had become interested in the professional side of acting. He joined his brother in obtaining representation.

Our oldest had also deepened his involvement in the arts.

He enjoyed sports and the team camaraderie they offered and continued to participate in those activities. But he had also shown an enjoyment of his piano lessons and had chosen to add guitar lessons into the mix. This was in addition to what was becoming a very active involvement in his middle school musical theater program.

This latest development had come as a pleasant revelation. At age ten, he participated in a summer camp program run by the school's musical theater department. He surprised us by coming home from auditions with a principal role. While his younger brothers had always sung and danced around the house nonstop, we'd never thought of our oldest as a musical theater kid. Yet it turned out that, for a time, he was. He'd always been able to carry a tune, but now, under the direction of vocal instructors, we'd discovered that he, too, was a singer. His natural coordination also meant he was able to pick up dance choreography quickly in spite of having chosen basketball over dance classes.

Though he had no interest in pursuing acting on a professional level, he was having a great time in his middle school program until he eventually hit a fork in the road. There wasn't enough time to do it all, and his schedules were beginning to clash. Ultimately, he chose to forgo travel basketball to create more time for guitar and musical theater —both of which still afforded him the sense of community and coming together to achieve a common goal that he'd had on his sports teams.

In just a few years, our sons had gone from casually dabbling in the arts to showing open passion for and dedication to various forms of the creative arts. At home, we were knee-deep in re-creations of the younger boys favorite musicals (complete with homemade costumes and elaborate staging), acting and dance classes, and, for our oldest son, guitar lessons that included student cover gigs in professional music venues. All three were taking piano lessons, and each had requested additional instrumental lessons and/or voice lessons. It was rare to enter our home when all three boys were present and not see or hear some type of creative output coming from various rooms in the house.

As we drifted more and more into the world of raising creatively driven offspring, I increasingly found that parenting stories from parents of kids who were not passionate about the creative arts didn't always resonate deeply with me. There were some similarities, but there were also emotional and logistical differences. It wasn't until I began to converse with the other parents waiting outside of lessons and rehearsals or in the audiences of various performances that I began to find my parenting compatriots.

It felt as if I'd discovered a secret society filled with parents whose stories of parenting were slightly different versions of my own. "Oh, I should have known. This one came out singing and dancing. Always putting on a show." "She's such a perfectionist about dancing—it worries me sometimes." "Even when she was little, we could take her anywhere as long as we brought a sketchbook and crayons." "One of my favorite photos of my son as a toddler is one where he's playing his toy guitar—upside down."

The stories of the challenges and triumphs they would discuss were familiar, and there were many common themes among the parents. They were all looking for the best way to support and relate to their teens' or tweens' experience, from finding and maintaining friendships in spite of differing interests or schedules to choosing the right instructors and the right program fit to managing perfectionism or perceived laziness. I had once again turned to searching for literature on navigating the teen and tween years with creatively inclined offspring, and now that I was looking for offerings directed at adolescents, I found even fewer options than I had when my boys were younger.

One afternoon, while waiting for a rehearsal to end, I became engaged in a conversation about motivation and perseverance with another mom. She mentioned that she wasn't fully convinced her daughter was truly invested in acting in musical theater, as she "refuses to put in the practice time on the parts she's not naturally strong in."

I questioned the mom's interpretation of her daughter's behavior and suggested some reasons why her daughter's actions (or lack thereof) might not be indicative of a lack of passion but perhaps something else more akin to fear of failure because she loved her art so much. I'd seen her daughter perform, and she seemed to exude joy when in shows, even during the tedious parts such as late-night rehearsals on top of full school days.

The mom stopped, looked at me, and said, "Wow. Thank you. That is so helpful. I never thought of it that way, and that would explain a lot. Whenever we suggest she not try out for a show if she won't prepare properly, she becomes borderline hysterical, telling us that being in the musicals means more to her than anything else. Being a therapist must be so helpful for parenting talent."

"*Parenting talent?*" The phrase stuck with me as a funny double entendre, even though the mom did not mean it in that manner. I tucked it away in the back of my mind and carried on.

As life with creatively driven offspring often does, the path I had thought I was on veered in a different direction when my middle son—the one who had begged to be allowed to pursue working with an agent—was cast as Young Simba in *The Lion King* on Broadway.

Had you told me years earlier that I would ultimately close the private practice I'd spent years building to temporarily relocate to New York and wait by a stage door while my nine-year-old son signed autographs, I would have fallen to the ground laughing. I'll be very honest, when he'd originally asked to pursue signing with an agent, part of why my husband and I had said no was because we saw that entire world as slightly off-center.

Okay, what I had really thought was "Nope. Those kids are weird. And their parents are weirder." Yet here we were, following where our kid led us in finding his joy. Which left me as the weird mom walking her child home from a theater in the middle of midtown Manhattan at eleven p.m. as if I had just picked him up from school. We had no regrets. This once-in-a-lifetime experience cemented the commitment my husband and I had to best supporting our boys in their dreams in whatever way we could manage.

Upon my return to Chicago, the boys' lives were crazy busy with all of their various artistic pursuits—so much for my grand plans of not allowing my kids to be overscheduled.

On the days where I questioned both my children's sanity and my own, the days where we juggled all the things and narrowly dodged meltdowns, I found myself wishing they'd come with an instruction manual. I found myself keeping a list of topics I thought might make a useful book someday—a book I thought I might call *Parenting Talent*, inspired by that memorable post-rehearsal conversation.

As with everything else, the auditions, lessons, classes, rehearsals, and performances came to a sudden stop when the COVID-19 pandemic hit in 2020. While the world became familiar with moving from in-person events to Zoom video calls, I had more than enough time to figure out the next steps for my career. I knew my goal was to merge our continued desire to support our boys in their creative pursuits while also addressing my desire to get back to supporting others.

Shortly after this time, the mom who had had an "aha" moment after we'd spoken about her child's refusal to practice reached out to let me know she had shared the topic of our conversation with another mom of a creatively inclined teen. That mom was struggling with her relationship with her content creator daughter and was looking for some guidance. She approached me and asked if I would be open to a few meetings regarding her daughter's art and creative aspirations. She indicated that she had a therapist for other issues but wanted more direct assistance for her relationship with her daughter so she could better understand and support her.

After we conversed, I felt confident that I would be able to help this mom move the needle on what was becoming a contentious relationship with her daughter around her daughter's art. She was able to make some significant changes in her approach with her daughter. Later, she shared my information with some others managing similar challenges with their creatively driven kids, as well as with an owner of an arts program she was associated with. The owner asked me to consult with her staff about some of the issues we'd covered with my client. I found myself entertaining periodic organizational consulting requests to discuss these and other topics.

Over time, I added the topics I was covering with clients to the *Parenting Talent* list (usually while, as usual, waiting in my car for someone to finish up some arts-related rehearsal). Eventually, this list morphed into a rough outline, and ultimately, it evolved into this book.

I'd like to believe one of the reasons people have enjoyed working with me is because I'm very honest. Even with all the education, training, and information I have at hand, when my boys push my buttons enough times, I am no different from any other parent.

Just a few highlights of some very real moments: I have found myself yell-lecturing my sons about how much money we're spending on lessons and offering up vague threats of stopping lessons if they don't practice. I've wanted to bang my head against a wall when one of my boys leaves learning a script until the last minute and I find myself questioning if their audition turned out as strong as it might have if they had started earlier. I've mostly resisted the urge to roll my eyes when I suggest that perhaps their failure to get "off-book" sooner indicates that they'd prefer to pursue acting as a hobby instead of at a professional level and I am met with protests of "No it doesn't. I *loooove* acting!" I have resorted to nagging when I know nagging has never worked, never will work, and only serves to frustrate everyone involved—yet there I am because, in my frustration, I've forgotten what I know and I just want my sons to *get stuff done*.

Parenting can be challenging on the best day, and it feels so much better to know you are not alone on your journey. Whether your teen or tween has a newly discovered interest in an art or has been at it for years and has embraced their art as part of their identity, you are not alone if you have found yourself wondering "How do I support and encourage this? How do I find the balance between pushing and teaching life skills such as commitment and hard work, while also allowing room for joy and the freedom to decide to let things go and have fun with their art?"

It is important to note early on that in no way do I see creativity as solely existing in the domain of the arts. It exists in all realms and, when one thinks of advances made in math and science, it's undeniable that creative thinking has led to breakthroughs in those fields. However, for the purposes of this book, I am talking about teens and tweens who love the creative arts. These are the teens and tweens who love acting, singing, photography, painting, drawing, videography, dancing, music, writing, architecture, social media content creation, printmaking, graphic design, jewelry making, clay work, fashion design, makeup design... you get the picture.

I wrote this book with the desire to provide useful, cohesive, and hopefully relatable information regarding creatively driven teens and tweens. Whether your teen or tween has developed into a dedicated hobbyist invested in learning more about their art, has embraced their art as their primary extracurricular, or is invested at a pre-professional level, this book is for you. It is the book I wish I'd had when I was looking for direction on how to best understand my boys' needs and desires with their various arts.

My boys all continue to enjoy creative pursuits and have all been labeled "talented" in various contexts. Whether or not they all choose to continue pursuing the arts long term has yet to be seen. My oldest is now a young adult and currently committed to a career connected to music; my middle cannot image not continuing his journey as a singer-songwriter and actor; and my youngest continues to act and play drums and has recently begun to teach himself guitar, but he still has plenty of time to decide if the arts will become his ultimate career path. For now, we are still a house buzzing with creative energy around every corner.

That fuzzy picture I had in grad school of what parenting and family life would look like has finally come into full focus. It looks different than I thought. There are, in fact, gear bags loaded into the trunk, but instead of being sports-related, the bags are full of music-related equipment. Though we do keep folding camp chairs in the car, they are most often used at outdoor concerts. The cheering is clapping, the uniforms are costumes, and the sidelines are performance venues. I am proud of myself for having embraced being a supportive, only *slightly* overbearing mom cheering my kids on from the audience.

This parenting journey and family life is better than I ever could have imagined, and I am forever grateful that my boys find joy in this world.

My husband and I work to encourage and affirm our sons in their wildest dreams. I am grateful that I have my training as a therapist to assist me in working to better understand and support my creative kids in their goals, both large and small.

If you are a parent, teacher, instructor, coach, or another person who cares deeply about a teen or tween creative artist, my goal is to help shed some light on how to better understand and try to make sense of teens' and tweens' connection to their creative pursuits. The ideas I share in this book are some of the concepts that assisted me in becoming a better steward of my boys' journey. Hopefully, as you read this book, you will find some inspiration, guidance, or even just solidarity in your journey of parenting talent.

Chapter 1

Creative Kids, Creative Concerns

Do any of these scenarios sound familiar?

• Is there constant live music playing in your home? Do you have a line item in the family budget that reads "music gear" to plan for the constant replenishment of drumsticks, guitar or bass strings, straps, cases, capos, cymbals, earplugs, and all the other seemingly never-ending supplies your young musician needs? Do you assume you will find guitar picks in your dryer? Do you count moving amps out of the way as part of your workout routine?

• Do you have days marked on your calendar when you will have to drive your teen to and from school because they will need their "good" tuba, bass, cello, cymbals, bass clarinet, French horn, or whatever other large instrument since it won't fit on the bus? Do you buy tickets to the high school football game just to watch the band? Have you had intense debates about whether marching band is a sport?

• Do you have a bin of ballet shoes, a sewing kit, and accessories next to the family shoe bench? Are leotards, skirts, wraps, and tights their own laundry category in your home? Is there a drawer in your vanity assigned to bun covers, bun builders, bobby pins, elastics, hairspray, and hair gel? Do you have a portable tap dance floor set up in your basement? Is it near a freestanding ballet barre?

• Did you long ago relinquish your laundry tub to paint smears, learn to maneuver around drying brushes perched precariously on the edge, and grow used to having various cleaning solvents stored behind the faucets? Do you have a standing order for canvases or sketch pads delivered monthly? Do you know what a micron pen is, and have you purchased more than you care to remember? Have you been grumbled at by a teen for grabbing tracing paper left on the kitchen table to jot down a note?

• Do you assume the family vacation will include a teen or tween yelling, "Wait, stop! This would make great B-roll for my channel!" and did you long ago make peace with being forced to wait while they video the landscape? Is a gimbal "must-have" equipment that is stored in your teen or tween's bag at all times? Does your teen or tween care more about Wi-Fi accessibility and upload speeds at a hotel than they do about the hotel pool because they want to make sure their newest videos are released to their channel on time?

• Do you hear constant singing ringing out from the shower, kitchen, family room, or whatever other room your teen is in? Have you found yourself purchasing both performance and recording microphones? Have you gifted your teen or tween an oversized vacuum-sealed water bottle so they can stay well hydrated before performances? Have you received texts from your teen while they were sitting two feet away because they were on vocal rest?

• Have you spent a large part of what should have been your retirement funds on camera gear you have no idea how to use but that your teen or tween is enthralled with? Does the equipment have its own high-end gear bags worth far more than any of your handbags? Are you grateful that your teen qualifies for the student discount for Adobe Suite? Have you invested in a computer for your teen or tween that is far more valuable than your own?

• Do you have audition dates and, more importantly, callback and cast announcement dates marked on your personal calendar so you are prepared for the emotional ups and downs you might see from your teen on those days? Do highlighters disappear due to scripts that must be memorized quickly? Have you been asked to run lines with your teen or tween and watched in amazement as they became a different person right in front of your eyes?

• Have you found yourself staying up late at night researching camps on Google using terms such as "fashion design," "architecture for teens," "intermediate animation," "graphic novel and illustration," "jewelry making," "storytelling," "advanced writers," "ceramics and sculpture," "songwriting," "sound production," "digital music creation," or references to any other myriad creative arts your teen or tween is passionate about?

While raising a creative teen can be one of the most fun, unique, exciting, and rewarding experiences out there, it can also be a confusing and confounding journey full of anxiety-provoking moments. It can bring up a roller coaster of emotions and a whole lot of questions.

Have you ever wondered about how to best support, nurture, guide, understand, and relate to your creatively driven tween or teen? Do you find yourself wondering what makes them tick? Do you notice yourself feeling anxious about a seeming disconnect between their professed love of their art and what, at times, may seem like a reluctance to engage with it? Have you been confused as to why they say they love what they do but won't put in practice time to improve? Or why they put tons of time into their art of choice, but refuse to share it in any public manner that may give them a moment to shine? Or perhaps it's the opposite, and maybe you've struggled with how to get your creatively driven teen or tween to moderate their focus on their art and find better balance with academics and other responsibilities.

Do you question how to help them flourish—how to help them be all they can be within their art? Are you concerned about walking the fine line of supporting versus pushing them? How do you hold them accountable? When is it time to step back and trust the process with their teachers, instructors, and coaches, and when is it time to listen to your gut and speak up when something isn't working—or worse, when it feels harmful to your teen or tween?

Have you been confused by your teen or tween's anxiety or their inability to believe in their skill set? Have you seen moments of vulnerability but not been sure how to comfort your teen or tween in an effective way? Do you worry about their resilience when faced with disappointment or bullies? Do you worry that they might lack community—friends who, if they don't understand the art, are at least supportive of your teen or tween's investment in it?

When, to my surprise, I first found myself parenting three boys who had all found part of their identity in the arts, I began looking for some guidance. My natural tendency is to be a researcher of sorts. I like to do deep dives into subjects that interest me, getting my hands on as many perspectives, theories, and models as possible to hopefully gain deeper insight. Of course, nothing interests me more than the emotional health and well-being of my boys. So I began reading all that I could, integrating it with the knowledge I'd gained in my education and practice, and talking—a lot—to other parents about their experiences.

This book is designed to help you gain confidence and clarity in identifying and meeting the emotional and practical needs of your creatively driven teen or tween. The information is aimed at offering you some new ideas and perhaps a fresh perspective on parenting and advocating for your artistic child. My goal is to help you to develop better communication strategies and to gain insight into where to step in, where to step back, and how to help your creatively driven kid make decisions and take agency in their relationship to their art. No one loves your teen or tween more than you do, and no one else will be willing to work as hard and sacrifice as much to help them achieve their deepest and greatest hopes and dreams.

As you read through this book, you will find that it is organized into three parts. Part I provides you with a framework for understanding how your teen or tween may approach their art. In this section, you will learn about some unique perspectives or challenges your teen or tween may face as a creatively driven being. I'll help you understand why your teen may be stuck in a pattern of loving their art but fighting new skills, and I will show you how to shift this dynamic. By the end of part I, you will understand how the way your teen or tween is wired to learn and think may impact their approach to getting things done (or not getting things done) and how this information can empower you as their parent to set them up for success.

Part II offers insight into some of the obstacles—both emotional and practical—that your creative teen or tween may struggle with as they work to explore, enjoy, create, and experiment in their art. Whatever your teen or tween is struggling with, from perfectionism to bullying to mental health to social media safety, you'll learn some practical starting points for traversing these obstacles to better support your young artist.

Part III covers some practical approaches and concepts that may assist you in integrating the material we've discussed into the practicalities of parenting a creatively driven teen or tween. You will learn how to embrace a parenting style that best meets the emotional and practical needs of your teen or tween, and by the end of this final section, you will feel equipped to navigate whatever your creatively driven teen or tween ends up deciding to do with their art in the future, whether they choose to consider it as a career or decide at some point that it's time to move on from their art for good.

Armed with the information provided in this book, I hope you will find yourself a little more enlightened, confident, and affirmed and a little less anxious, confused, or frustrated about the joys and challenges that come from parenting talent.

Part I

Understanding
Your Creative

Chapter 2

The "Talent" Trap

I was packing up after watching my oldest son's band play at an outdoor park venue. As I was gathering my thoughts and things, various audience members who'd come to watch these young men (who'd all attended various schools in our suburb) recognized my husband and I as our son's parents and walked up to congratulate us on the band's performance. The band had come prepared, had understood their audience, and had had a good balance between their originals and unique covers that the crowd had recognized and enjoyed. They'd been entertaining and funny and had spontaneously interacted with a toddler with a toy guitar who'd come to the edge of the stage, mesmerized by the live performance and imitating their singing, playing, and movement onstage. The band had shown their local community that this wasn't just a hobby; they had matured into a professional act. Chances were good that this performance had opened doors to larger gigs, potentially additional paying ones.

A mom of one of my son's former classmates came up to say congratulations. She commented that she hadn't seen my son in years and it was great to see him so confident, happy, and "in his natural element onstage." The last time she'd seen him perform had been years earlier, when he had held various roles in his middle school musical theater program. After middle school, he'd moved away from musical theater and had turned to his deeper interest, electric guitar. He also played keys and covered some vocals with his band, but he was always happiest when he was playing guitar. During this concert, many who'd only known him as a theater kid years ago got to see him engaged in his truest passion for the first time.

"Thanks so much," I responded. "He and all the band members really love what they do."

She then proceeded to ask me, "When does he head back to school?" In our middle-class community, many parents consider immediate matriculation into a four-college the assumed—or even required—path after high school. An alternate approach, especially for academically solid students, isn't one they automatically consider.

I smiled and said, "He doesn't. For right now, this is what he's chosen to pursue. His primary focus is on being a musician. He works for a music school and has some private students. He's figuring out how to make a sustainable income doing what he enjoys. He's taking a few college classes, but right now he's trying to figure out if they're necessary for his goals. We're so happy to see him thriving."

Her response was enthusiastic and genuine. "Oh, that's so great. He has so much *talent*—I'm sure he'll be successful!"

"Talent." It's a word that is used in our culture on a regular basis. When we see a better-than-expected performance, product, or presentation, our inclination is to comment on the *talent* of the individual who has impressed us. I've heard this applied to my own children as well as countless others we've witnessed throughout their creative journeys.

But what exactly is talent? And what if your kid doesn't have it? Oxford Languages offers this definition:

talent—natural aptitude or skill[1]

Sounds simple. Innocuous and obvious. Yet, ironically, given the title of this book, I'm not always a fan of the word —even though it's used by many as a sincere compliment. But the concept of talent, especially when discussing a young person, can be fraught with underlying expectations and limitations.

It's really the implication of the "natural" part that I have a problem with. There are, of course, people who are born with a natural aptitude for certain activities. Some skills and tasks come more easily to them than others. But acknowledging that someone has an innate ability in a creative field does not address the hard work and practice that continued growth of a skill requires. And this can be a dangerous oversight that has the potential to undermine growth.

We often label creative artists as "talented":

"She is such a *talented* painter!"

"He has such natural *talent* for design."

"What a *talented* budding chef!"

"You have such natural *talent* as an actor!"

While these statements are intended as compliments, they can take credit away from the artists' hard work. The word "talent" can imply that one does not need to work at developing a skill. We tend to assume that if you are talented in a certain area, all growth and development of that skill will just evolve effortlessly. The danger of buying into this idea is that, if the skill does *not* improve and progress effortlessly over time, well, perhaps you are not, in fact, *talented* in that area. Yet those whom we identify as the most talented in their art have, in fact, put in countless hours of skill building.

Growth and development in any area requires a certain amount of concentrated learning, work, and repetition of activities. My oldest son worked hard—very hard—to develop his skills as a guitarist. As a left-hander playing a right-hand guitar, he'd had to put in extra work to ensure that he reached the same levels of mastery as those playing with their dominant hands. As he'd gain ground in one area, he'd need to double back and work hard on another.

Mastered bar chords? Now work on finger speed and accuracy.

Finger speed and accuracy are improved? What about tone?

There is always something to learn, develop, improve upon, expand upon… and not all of the necessary skill development is easy, fun, or even pleasant. It's work.

My oldest son had also worked hard to appear effortlessly comfortable onstage. Many who praised his stage presence were surprised to learn that stage presence and performance had not always come "naturally" to him. He had had to work at those things. Part of his decision not to continue with musical theater had been influenced by the fact that the anxiety he would experience in the days leading to opening performances had been so unpleasant that he had no desire to continue to put himself through that over and over again for each new show.

No matter how much I would tell others that he could barely eat before each opening night, his confident, engaging performances would belie the anxiety he had experienced. To ensure this was how he came across onstage, he worked at it, and later he repeated the same work as a musician. Like many who perform, once he was performing he was fine, and, with music, he was having great fun. Yet getting to the point of being able to move, engage, relax, and banter onstage took work. Had he believed that "naturally talented" artists didn't need to work on multiple skills, he may have become discouraged and ceased to engage in the art he loved. Now he was enjoying the rewards of the internal work he'd put into finding his rhythm onstage.

There is a concept in psychology called locus of control. It references the degree to which you think you are in control of outcomes in your life. Those who approach life with an internal locus of control believe they can control—or at least guide—those outcomes through the choices they make and the actions they choose.[2]

Those who approach life from an external locus of control feel that outcomes are the result of outside factors over which they have no control. They believe fate, luck, and determinism explain success and failures in one's life. Had my son assumed an external locus of control based on whether he had a natural talent for feeling comfortable onstage, he would never have put the work into finding a way to feel comfortable. He would have avoided any performances that weren't mandatory and, instead of developing his skills in that area, he would have more likely become increasingly uncomfortable, perhaps to the point of avoiding public performance altogether.

In addition to this, implying that excellence is solely derived from talent can limit how motivated or open one is to trying something new that they may not demonstrate a natural affinity for in advance. If someone believes excellence can only come from talent, then if they would like to try a new activity but it does not come intuitively, they may believe there is little point in attempting to develop or master that skill. They may worry or assume it won't be possible for them to progress to a high level over time. Yet most of us know of many examples of people who worked hard to add new "talents" to their skill sets.

One of my clients, a bright young woman I have worked with since she was in her teens, tells a story of how she came to understand this distinction.

My sister and I are eleven months apart. My mother insisted we learn an instrument and started each of us in Suzuki violin lessons when we turned three. My sister took to it easily and quickly began playing recognizable tunes that were pleasing to listen to. Me? Not so much. I was the poster child for the "bad" beginner violinist with an out-of-tune, out-of-rhythm, wrong-note-filled recital performance. The difference was that, while my sister disliked violin and only played because my mother insisted, I loved it. I loved watching the sounds my teacher could coax out of the instrument when she would indulge me and play a short sonata at the end of a lesson. I love the vibration of the instrument on my chin.

At some point, the tables turned. My sister, who had been labeled the "talented" musician, was a competent violinist. She could read music, and she reproduced what she saw on the page in a manner that led to polite applause. On the other hand, I, who had put in countless hours past my mother's required thirty minutes per day of practice, became a skilled violinist. I understood the nuances of the instrument and was able to turn the notes on the page into something special, something that held an audience's attention. Suddenly I, a year younger and once labeled the "nonmusical" one, was being touted as the "talented" one.

I enjoyed the label and thought nothing of it until college, when I began teaching young kids for some extra cash. I watched the exact same dynamic that had occurred between my sister and me play out between a brother and sister, with the so-called "talented" sibling clearly marking time until she could go back to the soccer field and the "nonmusical" one loving every minute of his lessons. I stopped using the word "talented" as a teacher, and I started focusing on using terms like "effort," "hard work," and "improvement" to praise my students.

Another concern is, when a person hears they have "talent," they may see it as a challenge or test of their ability to bring that talent to every interaction. Instead of bringing out the joy and passion that could lead to continued skill development, these instances can turn into a gauntlet of expectations, perfectionism, and insecurity. Attempts to live up to others' expectations can quickly become destructive and detrimental.

I loved drawing. I'd always done it. My mom had me kind of young and most of her friends didn't have kids. I never minded being the only kid at a party, shoved in a corner while the adults were talking. I'd just bring my art pad and pencils and draw. I guess it kind of soothed me, you know? Like I could get lost in the drawing, telling myself the story of the character I was creating.

At one party, this guy came over and sat down to watch me draw. I remember being kind of creeped out by him at first, like why was he there? But it turned out that his sister was an artist and he was really surprised by my drawings. I guess he asked my mom if I'd ever had lessons and, when she said that no, she couldn't afford them so she'd never looked into it, he asked if he could have his sister call her.

So his sister, she worked for this really upscale studio in our town, but it turned out she also volunteered a few towns over in a less well-off area and they had a subsidized art program. She invited me to join and it was like, the best thing ever. I learned so much, and I really got a lot better really fast.

The lady who started me there moved, but she put in a good word for me at the other place she worked and they created a scholarship for me so I could come there tuition-free. It was amazing. They had every medium imaginable. I grew even more and was super happy. The director suggested I enter some stuff in some contests. At first, it was fun—especially when I won contests with money. But the problem was, for some [contests], winning meant I was automatically entered into bigger and bigger contests. And eventually, I wasn't winning that much. I wasn't placing at all, not even honorable mentions. And all you would hear was people saying, "Oh, there is so much talent at this showing!" and I kind of got in my head. Like, well, if there is so much talent here but I'm not even getting noticed, then I guess I'm not really talented."

It started impacting my love for art so much. I realized later, after I took a long break, that I had started creating art that I thought would win contests instead of art that I loved making in order to prove I was talented. And that took all the fun out of art—and it didn't work because now my art was like, you know, technically good but there was no real emotion behind it. Finally, I quit the studio and focused on writing. I did that just for fun and, when my English teacher asked to submit one of my short stories into a contest, I said no. I was lucky—when I explained to him why, he really got it and didn't push, and he told me just to keep writing for the joy of it. That's when it clicked. That was what had happened with art; I'd lost the joy of it. So I started working on some art stuff at home.

Eventually, I went back to the art studio and asked if I could work there in exchange for some classes, and the owner and I got to know each other better now that I was older. I was finally able to tell her what had happened, and she totally got it. She really encouraged me to keep going with art. I didn't know it at the time, but each time she'd encourage me to do something, she was really helping me create a portfolio for college applications. But because she never said that, I was doing stuff for fun, and I was willing to try new things and scrap projects if they didn't work. So, instead of feeling like I was working, I'd just had fun learning and putting a lot of hours into my work, and what it turned into was kind of what I'd been avoiding: a portfolio that showed off my art talents.

Labeling skill mastery, hard work, and excellence as a craft "talent" can trivialize the time, effort, and perseverance your creative teen or tween demonstrates as they pursue mastery of a passion, interest, or activity. Avoiding the word "talent" is not intended to take away from any natural aptitude your creatively driven teen or tween may have been born with. (As I said earlier, there is no denying that some people are born with a natural affinity for something.) Yet it is important not to negate the impact of skill development over time in helping your teen or tween achieve and maintain the outstanding high level of achievement they demonstrate. "Talent" alone doesn't do all the work, and the presence of "talent" doesn't mean that one doesn't need to work to develop their skills. If a person is told repeatedly, "Oh, you are *such* a talented artist," they may develop the expectation that any and all effort produced should be above average at the very least, if not exceptional.

Using talent to explain excellence and success leans into the idea of an external locus of control. You either have talent or you don't, and there isn't much you can do to change that. Adopting this mindset can take the pressure off of personal responsibility, hard work, and dedication. This belief undermines the purposeful, systematic, repetitive, deliberate practice that builds skill development.

Yes, your teen or tween may very well be super talented. But when developing a creative skill, avoiding burnout, and encouraging growth, "talent" isn't necessarily where it's at; what matters is your teen or tween's interest in and dedication to the art they want to explore even when it's challenging. So, for the purposes of this book, I use the term "Creative" in reference to your creatively driven teen or tween, and I do not use the word "talent." Whether your Creative was born with a natural aptitude for their art of choice or they developed it over time due to an interest in and eventual love for it, know that, if they are passionate about it, the sky's the limit on where it may take them.

I'd encourage you, the parent of a teen or tween with talent—henceforth known as a Creative—to also rethink how both you and your teen or tween use the word "talent." Creatives are capable, expressive creatures with the ability to turn a knack for an art into a skilled thing of beauty. Celebrate the work they put into their art and the joy they extract from it from this effort. If your Creative says, "My teacher says I'm a very talented writer," consider modifying a response such as "Of course you are!" to an alternative like "Yes, you are! You also work very hard at it."

Here are a few suggestions to encourage your Creative to shift away from an external locus of control (talent) to a more internal one (skill building):

• **Discourage the blame game.** Look for opportunities to take an honest look at what your teen or tween is doing when you observe blaming behavior. For example, using an absurd or exaggerated response may help them recognized when they are casting blame inappropriately. When my boys were younger, I would often give them "silly" responses to comments about avoidable minor injuries. If one of my sons came running to me after jumping on the bed and said, "I fell off the bed!" I might respond, "Well, tell the bed to stop dumping you on the ground!" To a tween who comes home complaining about a poor grade on a test I knew they didn't prepare for, I might say, "Tell your teacher to stop testing you on material they haven't taught you!"

   ○ One mom did this when her son didn't practice the assigned music enough for placement in a band he wanted to get into, saying, "Next time they should give you the piece they want you to play in advance." (Clearly they had—her son laughed and gave her a hard eye roll in response.)

   ○ Even if comments tinged with humorous sarcasm don't work with your Creative, these examples should give you an idea of what to look for and talk about. When your Creative jumps into the blame game, looking for external causes for situations where they could have had more control, validate the upset emotions, but, if you are able, also insert a gentle example of how they may have influenced the outcome themselves.

• **Practice failure.** We'll explore the value of failure a little later in this book, but for the purposes of helping shift locus of control, encourage your Creative to try something new, completely unrelated to their art, that they have a good chance of failing. People with an external locus of control assess situations and activities for the potential of failure. Find an activity or situation that they have no emotional investment in where they can learn to be okay with—or even laugh at—their failed attempt. If they are notoriously uncoordinated, see if you can get them to try a three-legged race—preferably with a partner with a great sense of humor. Laugh a lot. Talk about what they learned in the effort and what they might do differently in a subsequent attempt.

- ○ Try something small but totally new that they may struggle with at first but are likely to ultimately find success in doing. Small wins in things we know nothing about can build our "I can learn to do this" muscle.

- ○ One tween I worked with was truly stuck in a world of "I can't improve." I had the mom have her daughter make a list of three things she considered herself "bad" at other than her art. Her daughter listed "cooking," so I suggested learning to cook—just one very simple dish—as a starting point. The daughter agreed to work with her mom to learn how to bake a chicken, even though she thought it was "kind of weird" and didn't believe it related at all to learning her art. The first time she did it, her mother was readily available to answer any questions and was hands-on with her assistance. The second time, her mother held back and only gave verbal support, and the daughter managed largely on her own. By the third time, the daughter sent the following message to me via her mom: "Okay, I get what you are trying to teach me—just because I suck at something now doesn't mean I always will." Though she undoubtedly had already been given this message previously, she needed some practice at it outside of the context of her art so she could release herself from caring as deeply about the outcome.

We can increase our aptitude for something by working at

it. By becoming mindful of how your words hold power and by using those words to reinforce that your Creative is in control of the expansion of their skill development, you are encouraging them to develop an internal locus of control and to explore and navigate their art from a position of empowerment.

Chapter 3
Motivation for Creation

The concepts discussed in this book are only some of the considerations you should keep in mind when thinking about how to understand, nurture, and support your young Creative. Individual personality, life circumstances, family dynamics, financial considerations, support level, and opportunities within the community are just a few of the additional influences on the individual that impact the "how," "what," "when," "where," and "why" a Creative engages with, builds upon, and immerses themselves in their art. I have found, however, that there are concepts and frameworks that can help you understand and engage with your Creative with more clarity. In this chapter, we will explore these ideas.

L is so disorganized. I am always stunned that she does so well in school and with her photography. Her room is always a jumble of clothes and gear, and I just avoid looking in her backpack. It's funny, but she does take care of her photography equipment, I guess because we told her that we'd sell anything we didn't find put away properly—it just costs so much and I could totally see her getting distracted and leaving something somewhere or somehow stepping on it. But I don't know, somehow she gets it all done. I'll be losing my mind knowing she has an English paper to get done and thinking she hasn't even read the book—but she'll finish the book, turn the paper in, and get a good grade.

She's really, really good at photography. She started taking photos of stuff at school for fun and posting on her Instagram, and people started noticing. She now has a lot of jobs doing photography for our local theater, for concerts, and she's starting to do more stuff for other schools. I'm really proud of her, and I'm impressed because she's mostly self-taught. We did give her a class as a present when her work started taking off and she wanted to learn more techniques on Photoshop. But I really just don't understand how she's managing when she's just so all over the place.

I had to learn to stop trying to get her to use some type of organizational system. We were both just getting frustrated, and she is actually getting stuff done and has set up her own successful business.

We all have different thinking styles and different ways of receiving, processing, and expressing information. These thinking styles vary, but most of us have a preferred way of approaching how we organize our world. Our ways of acquiring knowledge, solving problems, and making decisions are all influenced by our thinking style.

GREGORC'S MIND STYLES

Understanding thinking or learning styles can also help you understand how your Creative approaches their art of choice. There are many models of learning styles. I found Anthony Gregorc's model, called the Mind Styles Model, very helpful in understanding how Creatives may approach their art. Gregorc divides thinking styles into four quadrants based on perceptual and ordering preferences.[1] His research focused on learners' mental strengths and abilities.

The Mind Styles Model is based on the idea that there are two continuums that form how we perceive and order information. Perceptual preferences run from concrete to abstract and ordering preferences run from sequential to random, leading to four categories of thinking styles:

• **Concrete perceptions** are made using the five senses. This is how we take in obvious information when we are not seeking connections or hidden information.

• **Abstract perceptions** are what allow us to understand things that cannot be understood through our five senses. This is where imagination and intuition come into play.

• **Sequential ordering** is taking information and placing it in a linear, logical organization.

• **Random ordering** is when we take information and place it in no specific order or in large general groups. Random ordering allows for the ability to skip steps and still achieve a desirable outcome.

By combining these two continuums, Gregorc developed four categories of mind styles (also known as thinking styles): concrete sequential, concrete random, abstract sequential, and abstract random.[2]

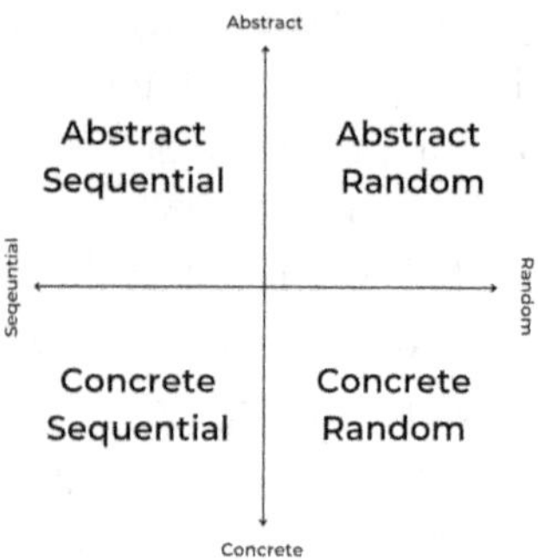

Each of these thinking styles has certain characteristics that impact how we learn. There is no one thinking style that is superior to the others. They are all highly effective in certain situations, and they all have weaknesses in others.

Oh my, my poor kid. So do you remember the show *Family Ties*? There was a character who was super conservative in this liberal family. My daughter reminds me of that. Not in a political sense, but the character liked things to be organized and based on research, and his parents were these two former hippies who liked to just kind of feel their way through life. So when M was little and started showing interest in the piano, we thought, "Great—she'll fit right in." We are an artistic family, and my husband and I have always been pretty laid-back in how we approach things. This works great for our other three kids; they seem to thrive on the chaos. But M, she hates it.

Her first piano teacher was a friend of mine who is like me, so she was also super laid-back and was more like a friendly grandmother in her approach. But M was always wanting more from her. She wanted someone to say, "You need to learn these three things, and if you finish that, you can go on to this." M started trying to teach herself extra stuff by looking ahead in her book. One day, she came home from a friend's house. The friend had a piano teacher who came to their house, and the mom had let M stay in the next room while they had the lesson since it was only thirty minutes long. M started quietly answering the questions the teacher asked and pretending to play on the table. The mom saw and suggested she just hop in on the lesson. M loved it. This teacher had her play something and immediately corrected her technique. M came home asking to switch. It was actually funny because what kind of happened was that the girls swapped teachers because her friend felt the teacher was too strict.

M thrived. She loved being told she had to practice scales for this many minutes each day and that she had to do other exercises for a certain amount of time. The kid would want to master everything she was given each week and would sit there methodically working through each lesson. No one believed me that I never had to tell her to practice. It's just who she is.

Now that she is a teen, we moved the piano into what used to be the reading room because it's small and not used a lot and M cannot stand when things are messy. She'd be picking up the living room before practicing, and we started to feel bad. It just didn't bother anyone else. So we gave her her own organized, clean room with her piano. She loves it there. She says she goes in there to relax.

Concrete sequential learners prefer to approach things in an orderly manner. They would rather use a logical approach based on facts and experience. They are happiest when they have the ability to engage in step-by-step processes or situations that have a high degree of structure. They are great at planning and organizing, and they may find disorder distracting.

Concrete random learners are more open to taking risks and being more creative in their approach. They may skip steps or miss some details as they rush to feed their curiosity. Concrete random learners like to experiment and may use intuition to guide their approach to new tasks. They are often divergent, curious thinkers who find creative ways to approach tasks.

Abstract sequential learners tend to be well organized in their approach. They are structured thinkers who like to debate and challenge concepts. They apply logic to their abstract thinking as they work toward solutions. They tend to be self-directed and enjoy analyzing new ideas and situations.

Abstract random learners are happiest in unstructured environments. They are imaginative, creative, and likely to make emotional connections with others. They dislike routine, orderliness, and mandated procedures and are happiest when allowed to approach things with a holistic, imaginative approach.

> As an art teacher, I wish someone had given me more information about learning styles and how to read the room based on my students. I'm a total abstract random learner. You know when you are young and you think everyone experiences life the same way you do? I mean, it's better now; young people hear about so much more with social media and stuff, so they have more insight into the idea that their experiences aren't universal experiences. But my generation was before all of that, even in college, and I just didn't really think about it. So when I started teaching, I thought all of the students would appreciate my super loose approach. My favorite instructors were that way, and I thrived when I had what I thought of as the freedom to figure out how to get to my end goal with some loose guidance.

I'd gotten mostly positive feedback, but then a mom approached me and asked if she could get a partial refund for her daughter who wanted to quit my after-school class. This girl was an incredibly gifted artist, and she always brought in any assignments I suggested (never insisted) they do between classes, and they were brilliant. I was upset and embarrassed, thinking I'd done something wrong.

Thank goodness my boss had been doing this forever and encouraged me to call the mom and ask for feedback. I was terrified, but I did it. And the mom was great. She said she'd been in the waiting room and heard me teach and knew I was an invested and kind teacher. And she told me her daughter's best friend loved the class, but that it was a joke between her and her daughter's friend's mom that if one of their girls liked a class, the other would hate it. She then went on to explain that her daughter preferred a much more structured class. She liked being told what and how to do something first, and then, once she mastered it, she would feel more comfortable "coloring outside the lines." She was happiest when she had homework that was broken into specific steps and when she received feedback on that work. The mom then went on to explain that her daughter was an ideal academic student and loved school and all the rules and structure, but, as much as she loved art, they had had a hard time finding a class that she really liked. Her favorite was a five-day camp at a college that was super structured—the teacher was used to college students and ran the camp like a class. "My daughter was one of the only kids who loved that camp," the mom told me.

It all made sense when I finally did a quiz on learning styles. It wasn't so much about finding out mine—I knew my own, even though I didn't have a term for it. But when I read about the other types of learners, a light bulb went on. So, after that, I kept offering the same class, but I split it into two sections. I was super clear on the descriptions: one section was for more laid-back learners, and one was for those who preferred more structure.

I wasn't convinced I was going to get a lot of students in the second section, but I reached out to that mom and she enrolled her daughter, and another one of her friends joined her. The structured section was smaller than my other section, but I loved teaching those six kids. They were sponges and, once they all understood what they were learning, no one minded if they raised their hands and asked super specific questions. They all did it. And I never worried if we didn't get through the entire lesson in the hour. I could just assign them homework and they'd walk back in with it all completed.

When I coach parents of Creatives, I find that, while many know about one or two learning or personality inventories, few are aware of the plethora of other tests and conceptual maps out there. Fewer still have heard of Gregorc's mind styles.

I've sat and watched a light bulb go off as a concrete sequential parent realizes they are raising an abstract random Creative. Once we've determined their Creative's mind style, it can serve as a road map in assisting and supporting growth.

Concrete sequential learners are most comfortable when they have the opportunity for direct, hands-on experience. They will respond best to an orderly presentation; they want to know what is expected and what is coming up next. The same meeting that their abstract random peer finds boring and tedious is enjoyable and soothing to a concrete sequential.

Two things any new dance instructor needs to know about G.

The first is that, if it's at all possible, she needs to know the stage she will be performing on in order for her to fully relax and give her best effort. She hates competitions for this reason; she never likes rehearsing in one space but performing in another.

The second is that she's the only one who can touch her dance bag. She has a very specific way of organizing her bag —it's meticulous—and it makes her crazy when people touch it. It really throws her off. I used to worry that it was a borderline problem, but then she said, "How would you feel if someone went into your computer right before a presentation and moved all of your slides around?" Then I got it: the stuff in her bag is part of her preparation to perform.

She actually now has a second small pouch that she privately calls her "DPP—Disorganized People Pouch." She got so tired of other dancers asking her for bobby pins, lipstick, Band-Aids, etc. that she made a separate pouch that she just hands them. Everyone knows G will have all the things, so they all go to her—often instead of the dance instructor.

Concrete sequential Creatives are punctual, prepared, and organized. As a parent, you won't find yourself reminding a concrete sequential to practice. They will have a plan and will execute without outside influence. One mom offered this example of the contrast between her daughters:

On competition days, C will be running around trying to find all of her stuff while M and I are already in the car waiting. M will have packed two days before. She will also have researched how long it will take to get to the facility at the time of day we need to get there, and she will have even factored in her sister's disorganization, telling her we need to leave fifteen minutes before we truly need to be on the road. She will figure in the time it will take to park in a new facility, find where they need to be, and register.

C will jump into the running car, laces hanging out of her bag, and then start doing her makeup in the back seat without a care in the world. C is very lucky her sister is so different; my husband and I both work full time but never worry about managing their dance schedule. M will update the family Google Calendar with all the relevant information so we can plan accordingly.

Concrete random learners are not concerned with making a good impression on others or trying to win others over. They are concerned with progress and achievement, but they aspire to those things more for their own gratification. Because they are focused on doing things in the most efficient way possible, they have little tolerance for engaging in activities they see as a waste of time.

Concrete random learners enjoy engaging in trial and error as a way to find the most expedient and effective solution. They love a good challenge and find obstacles as something to be traversed as opposed to an insurmountable block. They are often leaders and are most comfortable when they are the decision-makers. They are open to change and do not see the point of doing something a certain way just because that was how it was done before.

It's funny, at first we thought K didn't really like her videography camp. But boy oh boy did she change her tune after the first week.

The first part of camp was more structured, with everyone sitting at tables making sure the kids knew how to use the equipment and going over some more advanced editing, which involved very specific lessons. But then they let them film and edit their projects. That was when K went from being casually interested in filmmaking to being a passionate fan. She loved that she got to work on her own movie and figure out the best way to move a story forward. She loved being told to use her intuition and not necessarily do what was expected. She loved that she could try editing in different ways to find out what she thought was best. My kid also loves to compete, and she loved that there was an award for best movie at the end—which she won. Now that she's in high school, she's talking about going to school for cinematography.

Abstract sequential learners excel with image symbols and verbal communication. They have excellent communication skills and thus are often highly verbal. They are happiest when information is provided in an orderly manner, and they may dismiss any other form of presentation as a waste of time. Because of their abilities with written and verbal information, they like to read, listen, and use visual cues during skill development.

Abstract sequentials may waffle a bit in their decision-making as they weigh two sides of an approach or argument. They may be skeptical of information shared by those they don't see as experts, and they may hold back in engaging with those with points of view different than their own.

Did you know there is such a thing as architecture camp?

J was always the one who loved LEGOs. But as much as he enjoyed putting a set together the regular way, he really loved those LEGO idea books. He loved making his own things from the bricks he had.

My parents had J stay with them one summer, and they live near a university that offers camps for tweens and teens. On a hunch, my dad put him in architecture camp. He had the time of his life. The instructors adored him. He was the first to put his hand up, and he loved problem-solving and explaining his solutions.

The camp was very hands-on, which is how J learns best, and they gave campers a choice to work alone or in teams. J is that person who likes to work alone but in a room with others, so this was perfect.

My poor parents had no idea what they started. From that summer on, J wanted to go to their place every summer. Now that he's in high school, we let him stay in the dorms, and camp is the highlight of his summer. They know him now, so they basically let him go off and do advanced projects and they just mentor him—which is his dream situation. He's not always the most tactful when talking to people if he disagrees with them, so this setup really works for him because the adults are so impressed with him that it's the one place he can monopolize the conversation and it's appreciated.

Abstract random learners often lead with their intuition. They enjoy the less structured nature of group learning, and they tend to be adept at reading others' moods. They often see rules and expectations as limiting and prefer to experiment in various manners. They are often experienced by others as high-energy, and they rarely pass up an opportunity to socialize. Abstract randoms do not enjoy strict scheduled routines.

There are two jazz music programs near us, and we just randomly chose the one closest to our house. After a few weeks there, T said he didn't like jazz—he knew he really should learn some basics, but he just didn't like it, which surprised me because he loves to improvise and likes having the freedom to try new things.

Well, a friend from across town who was in the other

program asked T to sit in on a gig at the last minute. The instructor for the other program was there, and T just really liked him. So he asked if he could do a trial class across town. He's thriving there. The first program was much more structured and was focused heavily on music theory. The other one was much more collaborative and really focused on building relationships as musicians and learning to really listen to one another. T said it reminded him of acting improv games but for music. He loved that the learning was more spontaneous—like if someone did something interesting, the instructor would go back and talk about why it worked, what was happening.

In the end, I was right. T loved the freedom of playing jazz and, once he had that going, he was able to go back and learn some theory.

Understanding a Creative's learning style can be extremely helpful when trying to assist them in moving forward in their skills. For example, an abstract random learner may be more open to structured practice times if their need for social engagement is being met.

One of my clients came to me incredibly frustrated by the fact that her daughter would constantly declare that all she wanted in the world was to be an amazing guitarist but would rarely engage in any sort of consistent practice. She loved her contemporary music program when she was playing with a band, but getting her to work on her assigned songs and the fundamental skills she would need to improve had turned into a battle. When asked, my client's daughter couldn't pinpoint why she wasn't practicing as she did desire to improve. Her only response was "I don't know, I just don't like to practice unless I'm in the mood."

After I did some work with my client and her daughter, we discovered that she was an abstract random learner.

Though she desired the results of practice, she hated spending time alone in the basement where her guitar and amp were set up, and she hated being locked into a specific time to practice. My client and her daughter agreed that she could move her gear up to the family room off of the kitchen, and she could practice whenever she wanted as long as she was not disturbing anyone. My client later reached out to say:

> I'm still not totally believing this will last. Now she's practicing at least four days a week, and usually it's while I'm making dinner in the next room. She actually texted me to ask what time I usually start making dinner. I promise you, if I had told her she had to practice while I was around she would have refused, but this is working for her. She seems happier when there are people in the kitchen.
>
> My husband said she started practicing late one night while he was cleaning up in there, so he just decided to keep going and mop the floor since he was getting a live concert to work to.

If you are interested in learning more about your Creative's learning style and how to use this information to create a more effective learning environment tailored to their preferences, you can access a quick learning styles quiz at https://parentingtalent.com/creatives-learning-styles-quiz/.

PERSONALITY STYLES

Another factor in how your Creative engages with their art is personality style.

There are many different ways of categorizing personality styles. Many working adults are familiar with the Myers-Briggs, the DiSC, or the Enneagram assessment tools. The information gathered from these tests can be useful for understanding personal motivation and team building. I've seen many people have "aha" moments after seeing their results from these types of inventories and recognizing the relative accuracy of the description of how they navigate and interact in their world. Each inventory out there has its own usefulness in various contexts. In this book, though, we're going to focus on one I find particularly useful for understanding Creatives.

Gretchen Rubin is an influential writer on the linked subjects of habits, happiness, and human nature and is the founder of The Happiness Project. She created a framework, the Four Tendencies, that I have found to be extremely useful for those who wish to understand how teen and tween Creatives respond to demands and expectations around motivation and skill building in their chosen art. This framework has also been very helpful in my own journey as a parent of three Creatives, as each one of my boys has a different tendency.

I first read about the Four Tendencies in Rubin's book *Better Than Before*.[3] One of my boys was homeschooling at the time, and I was looking for some additional tools to assist him in building better habits around his schoolwork. I'd loved Rubin's book *The Happiness Project* and was interested in learning her thoughts on and approach to changing habits.

Though I was reading for one purpose, as is often the case, I quickly found the Four Tendencies framework to be a very useful framework for helping all three of my boys. In the context of motivation, approach, and progress, it made shifting my interaction with each of my sons more targeted to how they best made progress. After recommending the book to others, I've heard from other parents and instructors that they, too, have found that the tendencies helped them understand how to best move the needle on skill building.

Rubin later expanded this framework in her book *The Four*

Tendencies.[4] She proposed that everyone tends to fall soundly into one of four categories, which explain our *tendency* to respond to inner and outer expectations. The categories are as follows:

• **Upholders:** Upholders love rules, plans, and expectations. They are both self-disciplined and self-motivated. When you tell them what needs to be accomplished, they will make a plan and follow through. They meet both inner and outer expectations.

• **Questioners:** Questioners need to understand the reason behind and the purpose for requested actions. If you can offer a clear explanation for why something needs to happen and they buy into it, they will comply. They meet their own expectations but resist outer ones.

• **Obligers:** Obligers do well when they are being held accountable by an outside source. They prefer when others have expectations of them, which gives them a sense of purpose, and they are reliable team members. They meet outer expectations but struggle with meeting inner ones.

• **Rebels:** Rebels revel in their individuality and free choice. They do not want to be told what to do or be accountable to others. They defy both inner and outer expectations.

Once you have identified which of these tendencies your Creative falls under, it can help you understand how to best approach helping them help themselves with skill development within their craft.

Here's an example. An art student who excels in abstract art has been told by their art instructor that realistic drawing is an essential skill for reaching their full potential. Each tendency is likely to have a different response to this expectation.

• **Upholder:** "Okay. When can I start? Do you have a class you recommend? I'd like to get enrolled right away."

• **Questioner:** "Why? I don't really like doing realistic drawing, and if I'm not going to be focusing on that, how will it help me? Why can't I just do what I'm good at and work at getting better at that?"

• **Obliger:** "Okay. How will I know if what I'm doing is enough? Will you give me a list of goals you want me to achieve?"

• **Rebel:** "Why? I'm not going to. I do abstract art. Realistic drawing has nothing to do with my goals."

By understanding this, you can have a game plan in place to help your Creative embrace and progress on the necessary skill. Here's how you might respond to each.

• **Upholder:** "Yes, here's a list of resources. Let me know when you're finished and we'll go from there."

• **Questioner:** "It's an indispensable skill. It's been used in various periods of art back to cave drawings. It's considered a foundational skill for many types of art, including abstract art, and it will help you be a stronger abstract artist."

• **Obliger:** "Yes. Here are two different classes and a list of the skills you should master. Check in with me each week to let me know your progress. You can also attend open studio time, where an instructor will keep you on track and help you with any questions or concerns."

• **Rebel:** "Realism is considered a starting point for many styles of art. Abstract art is often about breaking all of the rules, but to effectively break them, you need to know them in the first place. If you are ready to take your creativity to the next level, you may want to see if you are able to do a really phenomenal realistic drawing."

Personally, I have three of the Four Tendencies represented with my Creatives. Knowing this has made a difference by helping me understand how to motivate them to follow through on skill building, not just in their arts but in other areas as well.

Chapter 4
Perfectionism and Procrastination

I know I made M nuts. But she just was driving my husband and me crazy. She claims she loves writing, and she's really really good. Her teacher recommended her to a camp at a university—but even with the scholarship they awarded her, it was still a huge stretch for our family financially. My husband was reluctant, but M begged... and begged... and begged. So I agreed to work some extra shifts so that she could go. She had to come in with three different brand-new, unedited essays to share. We kept reminding her about them, but she just wouldn't get them done.

I'll admit, I kinda lost it. Here I was, working a ton of extra hours, which doesn't just impact me, but my other two kids too... just to give this kid a chance to do what she loved at a level she wouldn't be able to in our area. And she was acting like it was nothing.

Three nights before we were supposed to take her to camp, my husband flipped out and threatened to pull her from camp. Well, she fell apart. Sobbing, screaming, begging, saying writing was the only thing that made her feel good.

We were baffled and asked why she had not written the essays as asked then. And she didn't have an answer. She sat down and did them, but I could hear her crying on and off in her room. And I felt terrible. But I didn't know what to do.

She makes it really really hard to support her. Because even though she says writing is the only thing that makes her happy, sometimes it feels like half the time she's actually miserable and hates what she writes, and the other half of the time, she's just refusing to write at all.

Have you ever watched your child refuse to practice, even when you and they both know a lesson, class, event, or competition is approaching?

Or have you witnessed the exact opposite, where your child becomes obsessively focused on preparation, to the exclusion of all other responsibilities, and you find yourself having to put limits on what they're doing?

These can be flip sides of the same coin: perfectionism. And although one side can seem to serve in the interest of skill development in the creative arts, both sides can have negative impacts when experienced to overwhelming degrees.

PERFECTIONISM

Perfectionism, in a broader sense, is a combination of high personal standards, often to the point of an expectation of flawless performance, combined with a tendency toward overly critical self-evaluation.

A little perfectionism can be a fantastic, adaptive internal motivator. Too much can quickly become a paralyzing, maladaptive shackle of unrealistic expectations. Not all Creatives struggle with perfectionism, but it is a trait that can become an obstacle for some.

Dr. Brené Brown, whom you may be familiar with as a well-known and well-regarded author and researcher, discusses this difference, saying, "Perfectionism is not the same thing as striving to be your best. Perfection is not about healthy achievement and growth."[1] She goes on to explain how people tend to use perfectionism as a shield to avoid feelings of blame, judgment, or shame.

Both those with a small touch of perfectionistic tendencies and those with a touch too much have high standards, but it's the motivation behind the standards that distinguishes how those standards are experienced and expressed by the perfectionist.

This is an important concept when thinking about how someone approaches skill building in a creative art. Though skill building and experience through practice, performance, or other means of putting art out there are necessary for learning and growth, if one gets caught in too much perfectionism, it can lead to paralysis and prevent movement.

Researchers have established three types of perfectionism: self-oriented perfectionism, socially prescribed perfectionism, and other-oriented perfectionism.[2] All three of these types may be at play when your Creative becomes stuck in the process of exploring the medium they claim to love.

Self-oriented perfectionism is when we place an unrealistic desire to be flawless on ourselves.

Adaptive self-oriented perfectionism is when there are high standards for our output, but they are realistically high standards. Instead of thinking "I expect to get perfect scores at this competition," a Creative who is an adaptive self-oriented perfectionist is able to think "I hope I place in first, second, or third place." This reframing from an expectation to a hope, from a limited acceptable outcome to a broad range of valuable outcomes, keeps the desire to do well in an adaptive range. Furthermore, if the Creative comes in fourth place, they may be disappointed, but they are able to accept this as a very good outcome without judging themselves in a negative light or seeing this as a failure. They accept and learn from imperfection. They are open to suggestions and embrace them. They enjoy the process of learning and accept that mistakes are part of learning and improvement. They embrace feedback as a tool to become better.

In *maladaptive* forms of self-oriented perfectionism, Creatives set unrealistic goals or standards for themselves. They will approach tasks as black-and-white pass/fail endeavors. They are more likely to think "I have to win this competition to prove I am good at what I do." When presented with a fourth-place finish and excellent feedback, instead of embracing the positive comments, a maladaptive self-oriented perfectionist focuses on the idea that they lost or failed. They may beat themselves up and judge their abilities harshly. These negative critical self-evaluations are often motivated by fear of making mistakes.

Socially prescribed perfectionism is when we have the perception that others demand perfectionism of us.

Adaptive forms of socially prescribed perfectionism allow Creatives to view feedback from others as an opportunity to learn and grow. They use feedback, correction, and constructive criticism as tools to improve. They incorporate the new information into how they approach tasks.

Maladaptive socially prescribed perfectionists believe they are being judged negatively by others. They falsely assume that others are expecting a flawless performance and that any flaws will overshadow any positive output. Feedback, correction, and constructive criticism are all heard as evidence that their entire output was poor quality, worthless, or insignificant. Regardless of how this feedback is presented, these Creatives judge themselves harshly and consider the feedback as proof of a character flaw, lack of talent, or inability to improve.

Other-oriented perfectionism is when we tend to set very high, often very unrealistic, expectations and standards for others.

Adaptive other-oriented perfectionists can derive an increased sense of meaning and accomplishment when successfully performing tasks with others. When they meet or exceed the high standard they have set for those around them, they can feel satisfaction in their personal accomplishments as a result. They will think "I held my own with this group, and they are the best of the best."

Maladaptive other-oriented perfectionists are very critical and judgmental of others and will often alienate those who are trying to help them or work with them. They tend to be very critical when people are unable to meet their expectations and standards and they tend to question others' capabilities. For Creatives, this can lead to undermining and destruction of their relationships with instructors and peers and may permanently damage relationships. Maladaptive other-oriented perfectionists may think "My instructor didn't go to the top school in their art, so I'm not convinced what they are telling me is truly helpful."

Adaptive Perfectionist	Maladaptive Perfectionist
Open to asking for help or guidance	Avoids asking for help from others
Recognizes their own strengths and weaknesses	Expects to be good at all aspects of a task and sees mistakes as character flaws
Understands that improvement requires effort	Looks for immediate success and sees anything less as proof of complete failure or inability to improve
Makes plans to complete tasks effectively	Procrastinates and misses deadlines, then must rush at the last minute and cram to complete on time **_OR_** works obsessively without appropriate breaks
Has high standards but accepts that outcomes may not be perfect	Sets unrealistically high expectations for outcomes
Adapts as a means to improve outcomes	Rigid in their approach

For a perfectionistic Creative, regardless of the type of perfectionism they fall into, maladaptive perfectionism often presents in one of two ways.

Some Creatives enter an obsessive quest to avoid negative outcomes by practicing, revising, editing, and/or even completely abandoning and restarting tasks if they begin struggling. They may demonstrate poor time-management by pursuing perfectionism in a specific area to the neglect or exclusion of other responsibilities. They will overwork, often past the point of exhaustion, and will find themselves unable to relax or enjoy other activities until they feel they have mastered the task they are focusing on. They may present as anxious, controlling, stressed, or overwhelmed. The process of practice and preparation does not alleviate these feelings— and sometimes, paradoxically, the more they master the task at hand, the more critical they may become or the more they may doubt that their output will be "good enough" for others.

This approach may also lead a perfectionistic Creative to overthink or to overcorrect small mistakes. They may hyperfocus on small details that are of little or no consequence, or they may agonize over decisions, becoming paralyzed in self-critical loops. This misuse of time and energy can leave Creatives feeling as if no progress has been made in spite of hours of effort.

For other Creatives, maladaptive perfectionism will present as procrastination. They avoid the possibility of failure or of not being good enough by not engaging in or completing certain tasks. They may fantasize that, if they leave those tasks to the last minute, they can use the time leading up to the deadline to mentally prepare and produce a perfect outcome. Or, from an opposite approach, they avoid thinking about what they have to do because of the psychic discomfort of the idea that they may not be capable of a perfect outcome.

The higher the stakes, the more they may procrastinate. They may embrace the feeling that it is much safer to be able to tell themselves they didn't do well because they didn't try as opposed to feeling that their efforts were not enough. Although it may appear that the Creative does not care or is not invested in the outcome, the opposite is very much the truth. Underlying the seeming indifference lurks great anxiety.

All of these only serve to create a self-fulfilling prophecy where a Creative doesn't prepare for their task and thus does not improve at or master their skill and then experiences a less-than-ideal outcome. The very thing that would have increased their chances of a better performance, product, or outcome—preparation—has been sacrificed.

I don't know why I can't just get it together and practice like a normal person. It makes my mom so mad. I'll want to go out, and she'll say that that's fine as long as I practice first, but then I won't really be in the mood or I'll feel like I don't have enough time to do it well or I'll get distracted. Then it'll be time for me to go out, and my mom will be mad because I never practiced, but I'll promise her I'll do it when I get home. And then I don't. And then all of a sudden it's like I know my lesson is two days away, so I'll practice for four hours and get so frustrated because that's not a really good way to get better, and I'll be yelling at myself for being so stupid and not just practicing a little each day like my teacher and my mom want me to. And I'll be so mad at myself that I won't even want to try practicing at all the next day. But then my mom will ask if I even want to keep playing piano and I'll freak out because I do love piano. I'm pretty sure that's what I want to do in college. I just don't like making mistakes, and that makes it hard to practice.

SHAME CYCLES

Shame is a very powerful emotion that arises from internalized negative beliefs about ourselves. When experiencing a situation that leads to feelings of shame, we may feel we are bad, worthy of contempt, flawed, or otherwise inadequate as people. When feelings of shame arise, we may experience increased embarrassment, self-criticism, powerlessness, worthlessness, and self-consciousness.

Perfectionism and shame usually occur in tandem, often leading to a shame cycle where a person becomes stuck in an ineffective loop.

Here are some examples of a general perfectionism shame cycle:

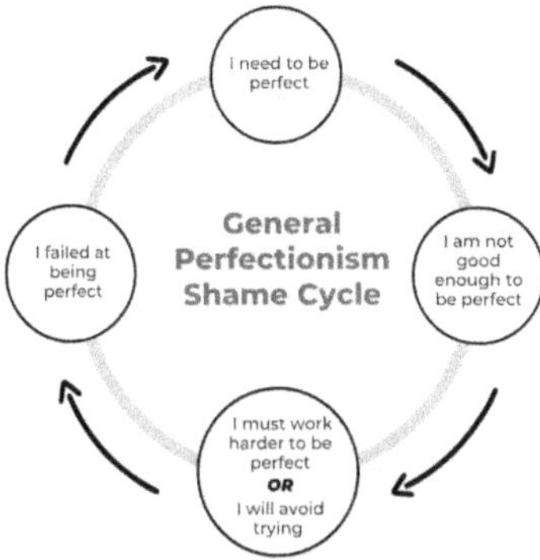

There can be variations on this theme depending on how the perfectionist copes with the anxiety and fear of not being perfect. For example:

Obsessive Worker Procrastination

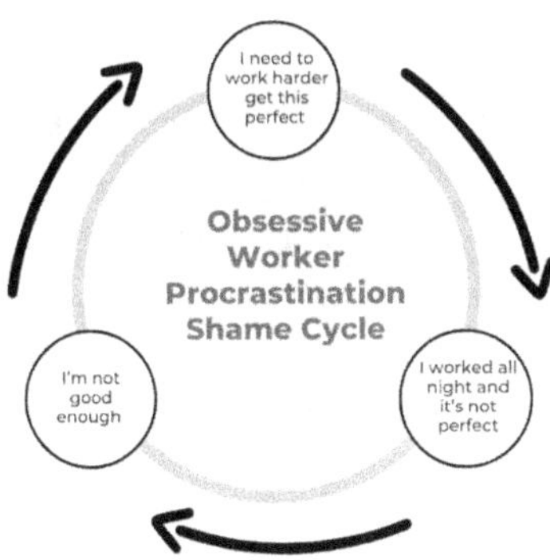

Avoidance Worker Procrastination

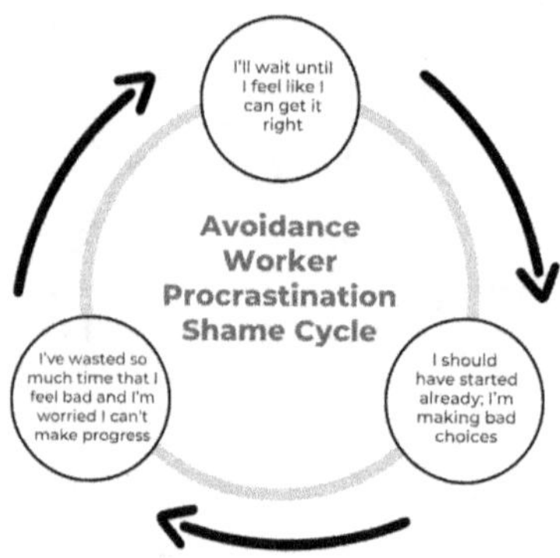

Binge Worker Procrastination

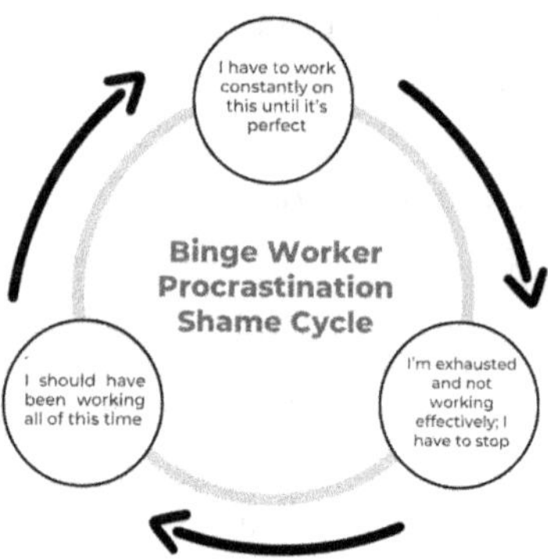

These shame cycles can spin tighter and tighter until the Creative feels hopeless to make progress. They may be stuck aiming for an unrealistic goal and find themselves unable to move forward. The cycles may also serve to keep them from trying new things and developing new skills out of fear of failure.

Another notable aspect of shame cycles is there can often be an acting out or anger component as the shame sets in. Shame feels bad and can be overwhelming. Expressing it as anger or acting out in a negative manner displaces some of the internal shame onto an external target. If you have ever had an angry Creative yell at you for reminding them of a deadline or obligation, you may have come up against this. When poor self-care—such as lack of sleep, poor eating habits, overscheduling, and other negative behaviors—comes into play, the acting out may be aggressive or hurtful to those around the Creative.

It's kind of a miracle that my sister and I are getting along better now. She was a nightmare. Night. Mare. We'd always know when a show or competition was coming up. She'd spend all day doing stretches in all of these weird positions. I got used to not walking through one of the doorways to our TV room because she'd be watching TV in the doorway, using it to make her stretch into an oversplit. She'd bite your head off if you said anything.

I started to really, well, hate her. We'd all be tiptoeing around because nothing you said to her was okay. If she was finally just relaxing and you said, "Oh, I'm glad you took a break," she'd respond with something like "Yeah, I get it, you think I'm lazy?" Like, what? That's not what I said.

When it was time for her to audition for her summer dance intensives, I'd want to just stay at friends' houses. She was impossible. It was all or nothing, super up, super down, super intensively rehearsing, eating a whole pizza then calling herself fat.

One time she actually hit me because I borrowed a sports bra from her. She was screaming that it was the one she was going to use in her audition, so she had to practice in it. Just so you know, she had like ten of the same style, so yeah, how was I to know that that one was "special"? And for the record, we shared clothes all the time.

I was done after that. So were my parents. They finally let me move my bedroom to the basement, away from her, and made her get therapy. It was sad because she could be a really good sister when there was nothing other than her normal ballet classes going on. Like, once she snuck out and took the car to get me from a party I wasn't supposed to be at when my ride started drinking and if I walked I would have been late for my curfew.

Her therapist did help some. Stopped her bouncing back and forth from not rehearsing to obsessively rehearsing. Now that she's at college, we get along so much better. Let her roommate deal with the crazy when she has an audition. I like her a lot more now when she's home on break and she's not feeling guilty about not rehearsing.

This shame cycle can ultimately lead to poor self-esteem. The feeling that they have failed can erode a Creative's self-worth and lead to anxiety and depression. But addressing perfectionism in a teen can be a challenge. When you do so, they may feel you are not being supportive, not under-standing how deeply they want to improve or prove them-selves to others. Some suggestions for addressing and managing perfectionism in your Creative teen include:

• Praising effort, not outcome,

• Demonstrating self-compassion through example,

• Helping them set realistic standards and goals,

• Assisting them to identify what they can control,

• Encouraging healthy risks in activities they are not as invested in, and

• Teaching risking and accepting failure through example.

These are only a few suggestions for helping your teen shift away from perfectionism (and the procrastination that comes with it). As you make your way through this book, you will come to see some common themes emerge around how to best support your teen or tween Creative while creating an environment that encourages a healthy approach to their art.

Chapter 5

Mindset, Fear, and Anxiety

When a creative teen or tween beseeches us to pursue an art they profess to love, we are looking for them to come to approach the endeavor with commitment and discipline and to, over time, increase their self-confidence—especially when (our) money is involved. Yet frequently, we adults do not see these things happening to the degree we'd hoped for, even when our Creatives are screaming from the rooftops that they love what they do.

This can become a more significant point of contention as Creatives become older and begin to make decisions about future career goals. Though your Creative may declare they are committed to incorporating their art into their further goals, you as a parent may be confused if you witness reluctance or even refusal to pursue the elements necessary to make progress toward this aspiration.

It is easy to confuse the lack of consistent commitment, self-confidence, and discipline with a lack of desire or passion. The resistance often comes from other factors that are undermining a Creative's ability to push themselves to excel in spite of a true desire to do so.

As discussed in chapter 4, perfectionism may be coming into play. Perfectionists are often looking for the perfect situation and the perfect outcome to feel in control—and shifting to focus to more realistic goals and channeling perfectionism into things that move the needle forward can be helpful. Understanding mindset can help you support your Creative in accomplishing this.

MINDSET

Dr. Carol Dweck has spent her career researching learning, success, failure, motivation, and resilience. Over time, she developed the concept of mindset theory. Mindset is one's internal set of beliefs about their intelligence, learning, and ability to learn new skills. People have one of two approaches to life's challenges: a fixed mindset or a growth mindset. A **fixed mindset** is the belief that your skills, abilities, and intellect are rigid. You are born with these traits and skills, and you are incapable of changing them. A **growth mindset** is the belief that you can influence or mold your natural traits through perseverance, drive, and thoughtful effort. Encouraging your Creative to embrace a growth mindset is preferable to a fixed mindset, as it allows them to move past obstacles when faced with challenging situations or learning new skills.[1]

Creatives with a **fixed mindset** assume skills, ability, and intellect are static. They may avoid new challenges or give up easily on new pursuits as they feel their efforts to master them are pointless. They may be threatened by the success of others, and they may fear criticism because they feel that they are helpless to use the information to their advantage. When feeling inadequate on the inside, they may simply refuse to engage in an activity for fear of looking inadequate on the outside.

Another concern for Creatives who approach life with a fixed mindset is they often confuse what they are *doing* with who they *are*. So, if they are failing to learn something, they may see themselves as a failure in their art. Learning to cultivate a growth mindset instead can be a game changer for a Creative who is feeling they are "failing" in their art of choice.

> You know, J kind of fell into a part in a community theater musical. They needed a young kid, and my sister, who was the assistant director, asked if he could do it if she would get him back and forth. He loved it and wanted to perform in more musicals. So I signed him up for our local kids' theater, and he almost always got a major role. But then we moved to a much bigger town, and this town had this crazy good musical theater program in the middle school.
>
> At first, J was so excited. There hadn't been a lot of theater boys in our old town. But he came home from tryouts looking miserable. He said that everyone there was a better dancer than him. I reached out to the director, and she said he had done fine. She said that many of the other kids had been in this program since they were in fourth grade, so they knew what to expect and had been learning choreography on the fly since then. She told me off record that he was getting a part because he had great stage presence and a great voice, and she suggested that he take some dance classes. So we signed him up, but he couldn't seem to get past not being in the same place as the other kids. He kept saying he "can't" dance even though everyone could see he had a sense of rhythm and was getting better. He even said he should just switch to regular plays, not musicals, because it was "hopeless." It was so frustrating because we could all

see him improving. The director was amazing and told him how impressed she was by his improvement, but he had it in his head that because he wasn't the best right away, all hope was lost and he was "bad."

On the other side of the coin, a Creative with a **growth mindset** believes new skills can be developed. This, in turn, motivates a desire to learn—to embrace challenges and see mistakes or setbacks as opportunities to learn and push forward down the path to mastery. People with growth mind-sets learn from the success of others and find lessons in those experiences to utilize for their own progress. They are open to constructive criticism, as they experience it as infor-mation designed to improve their skill development.

When working with Creatives, it's important to look at how they are approaching their art. In most instances, are they approaching it with persistence, enthusiasm, and, when needed, discipline? Do they have a sense of determination when faced with a new challenge or opportunity? Are they generally enthusiastic about classes, lessons, rehearsals, and camps, and are they able to find value in most situations? These signs of a growth mindset will be invaluable assets as they progress through the developmental phases of their art of choice.

L is just, well, fun. She is one of those people who is willing to try anything and can laugh at her mistakes. Her voice instructor was putting on a showcase, and L had never really performed in front of anyone. Well, sure enough, it kind of became "if it could go wrong, it did."

It started when she forgot her music for the piano accom-panist. But she didn't get upset, she just borrowed her friend's guitar because she'd practiced a few times that way. She had to sit to play because she'd worn these big high clunky heels and she wasn't comfortable playing and singing and standing. She lost her place... you get the picture. To make it worse, all the other singers were pretty polished. I was worried she'd be upset, but in her usual bouncy way, she just said, "It was fine. I mean, I know I kind of messed up, but now I know what to expect—you know—like what not to do. Like, I will never wear those shoes if I'm going to play and sing, and, yeah, I should have made sure I had a copy of my music on my phone. I'll totally do it again because if it was that much fun this time, it'll be great when I do all of that—oh, and [her instructor] was right, I should have practiced in front of a mirror—I'll do that for sure next time."

In chapter 2, I explained why the word "talent" has the potential to be a charged label for a Creative. With an under-standing of a fixed mindset, you can see how the word "tal-ent" may go hand in hand with fixed mindset. There can be an idea that you are either talented or you are not. The word "talent" can imply that you are either good at something or you are not, and it can lead to a false equation in your Creative's mind that if they are "not good" at something, it can't be changed, and if they are "good" at something, then they don't have to work hard to learn. This removes the motivation to work on skills to master competence, and it halts skill development. It's necessary to have a growth mindset in order to move forward while building new skills.

Martin M. Broadwell, a management trainer, developed a model of learning, or competence, that he called "the four levels of teaching."[2] Noel Burch used it as a manager at Gordon Training International, renaming it "the four stages of learning any new skill" (also known as the Conscious Competence Ladder), leading to more widespread recogni-tion.[3] While initially just four phases were listed, a fifth level has been added over time.[4] These five phases of competence in learning a new skill are:

1. **Unconscious incompetence:** You don't know what you don't know. Ignorance is bliss.
2. **Conscious incompetence:** You are aware of what you don't know. You are tuned in to what you need to learn.
3. **Conscious competence:** You start to understand how to do the new skills, but you are inconsistent. The new skills are hard and challenging, and you have to think about them as you do them.
4. **Unconscious competence:** The skills are now automatic and habitual. You can engage in the skills without thinking about them, and your mind may wander to other things without impacting your performance. It's effortless.
5. **Conscious unconscious competence:** This is a state of seamless flow and mastery, the ability to perform the skills at an exceptional level. Not all skills will reach this phase. At this level, you can explain and teach the unconscious components to what you are doing.

It can be helpful for Creatives to understand that even the masters they look up to go through this learning process—that those who seem to excel at a skill have to work through this process repeatedly as they tweak and improve on various parts of their skill development. If your Creative is approaching their art with a fixed mindset, they are not embracing the natural cycle of growth, which, at its core, requires an acknowledgment and embracing of incompetence.

When the Creative is able to acknowledge that incompetence is a natural part of skill development for everyone, it is easier for them to give themselves permission to be bad at something. It is in this very acknowledgment where the space to improve upon a skill in a more expedient manner occurs. This mindset shift is an important skill in and of itself. Learning to accept or tolerate incompetence, lack of mastery, and, yes, failure can be the leap between being okay to good or between being good to great.

So why do so many Creatives find themselves holding on to a fixed mindset—even in an era where teachers, coaches, instructors, and camps discuss and encourage a growth mindset?

FEAR

Fear is a natural, powerful, and primitive human emotion. It is the human reaction to a perceived threat, real or imagined. It is a combination of two reactions—the physical and the emotional. Evolutionarily, fear evolved to keep us safe. When presented with a threat, our bodies automatically prepare to keep us out of harm's way.[5] Our heart rates increase, adrenaline begins coursing through our bloodstream, our pupils dilate, and we may begin to sweat. Our bodies are preparing to engage in fierce combat or run as fast as possible away from the dangerous agent.

This automatic response—fight or flight—makes sense if you think of prehistoric humans. If heading into an unexplored cave for shelter leads to an encounter with a bear of similar inclination, survival would require an ability to fight or flee from the bear successfully. In fact, in modern times, we still hear about how the fight-or-flight response has saved lives. Parents fight off wild animals who have attacked their children; hikers survive falls and, even while severely injured, walk to safety; and strangers lift impossibly heavy objects off others to save their lives.

The emotional side of this response is more personal. Some people enjoy the feeling fear creates. They may love scary movies, seek out the highest, craziest roller coasters, and desperately want to try skydiving. They thrive on the physiological reaction to fear and find it to be a positive experience. Others find fear a negative experience and will work very hard to avoid fear-inducing situations.

Fear is a complex emotion, one that can have many triggers, but Creatives may specifically find they fear the unfamiliar when presenting their art. Unknown outcomes of future events (or even imagined events) may trigger a physiological fear response, and those who do not enjoy the fear experience may go to extremes to avoid or quiet the feeling of fear inside them when learning new things or facing new situations or challenges.

Adding to this is the very real phenomenon of fear potentially becoming an increasing issue as your Creative begins to gain skills, recognition, and success in their art of choice. As they climb higher in their art, they also have more to lose if they falter. This is where the work inside of mindset can become a powerful tool to help quell the fear response. Simply telling someone not to experience fear is no different than telling them to stop feeling tired. When a Creative has fear around new experiences, taking on new challenges, or learning new skills, the work must be done on a deeper level. It takes a lot of work and mental muscle memory to flip the fear into a growth opportunity and embrace the process of turning incompetence into competence.

ANXIETY

We are living in a time with unprecedented amounts of anxiety in our teens and tweens.[6] Just like fear, anxiety is a normal response to stress, apprehension, dread, or uneasiness about a situation or an event to come.

As teens and tweens age, they tend to move from concerns about external events or situations—such as fear that something bad will happen to a parent or worries about whether their new teacher will like them—to internal ones.

Anxiety tends to be a diffuse feeling of apprehension. When a person is asked what is causing them to feel anxious about a situation, they may not be able to articulate a precise or known reason. Among other symptoms, a person struggling with anxiety may report being unable to think clearly, feeling overwhelmed or restless, or having racing thoughts or a sense of doom and fatigue, in addition to physical symptoms, such as a racing heartbeat, sweating, upset stomach, or shortness of breath.

In Creatives, this may look like perfectionism—they may feel anxiety about the potential of producing a poor product or not doing well during a performance or competition. This may also present as concerns that others will not like them or what they create, that they can't live up to expectations, or that they won't be able to remember how to perform skills that are in their zone of unconscious competence.

It may also be expressed as irritability, poor concentration, sensitivity to criticism or feedback, withdrawal from their art, a decrease in the performance level of their art, or repeated reassurance-seeking.

Fear and anxiety are often generated from your teen or tween Creative's inner critic—that voice that expresses criticism, frustration, and disapproval about our actions. Self-critical judgmental or controlling thoughts can work to create fear of moving forward or anxiety about failing and can rob a Creative of motivation. Avoidance can create an illusion of safety while simultaneously creating a sense of shame and paralysis.

Building skills to quiet the inner critic takes time. Learning how one's inner critic is the voice of fear or anxiety and acknowledging it as such is one of the keys to embracing a growth mindset. If your Creative is able to see that their inner critic is trying to keep them safe but in fact is not helpful, then they can use this knowledge to push forward in spite of fear and anxiety.

In order for your Creative to better limit and control their inner critic, one of the first things they must do is become aware of it. Dr. Aaron Beck, a psychologist who developed pioneering theories related to depression and anxiety, used the term "Negative Automatic Thoughts," which Dr. Daniel Amen renamed "Automatic Negative Thoughts," or "ANTs."[7] ANTs are the negative interpretations we have of what we are doing or what we believe is happening to us. They can become a filter through which we run all of our experiences, impacting our mood, our feelings, and our relationship to activities and to others.

Evolutionarily, this tendency actually functioned in a useful manner. Keeping our minds alert to threats even when there were no immediate or obvious concerns kept us safe. The same was true for working to anticipate threats. If our imagination could warn us of potential negative results of our actions, we could work to avoid those results or could come up with solutions in advance.

Unfortunately, this ability to imagine the worst-case scenario is not as effective in the much safer world of today. Creatives, who often have heightened imaginations, may move into generating these ANTs on such a regular basis that they become habits. One study from Stanford University by

Dr. Fred Luskin found that nearly 90 percent of human thoughts in the course of one day are repetitive.[8] Imagine the impact of these thoughts if they are repetitive *negative* thoughts!

The human brain likes shortcuts. The more we do something, the more likely our brain is to develop a shortcut, an established pathway we use over and over. The more we use that pathway, the stronger the connection becomes, making it harder and harder to shift our minds in a different direction. Whatever we were repeating becomes a habit. And we all know that habits are hard to break.

Hard, but not impossible.

Becoming adept at identifying these ANTs is one of the keys to changing this pattern. Some things your Creative can try when working to shift away from ANTs include:

• Recognize black-and-white thinking cues such as "always," "never," and "all" or "every" and assess their truthfulness. Is the statement "I always mess up the shading when I use charcoal" actually true? Doubtful.

• When a situation seems negative, look for the positives—the silver lining. "Even though I didn't do as well in the essay contest as I'd hoped, I got some great feedback, and I know what to do differently next time."

• Don't assume you know what others are thinking—you are not a mind reader. When not cast in a desired role, jumping to the thought "The casting director thinks I'm not a strong enough singer for the role" is a negative assumption. There may in fact be—and there often are—dozens of reasons why casting choices are made.

• Avoid "shoulding" yourself (it is rarely motivating for

change), and change "shoulds" to positive self-statements. Shift "I should practice more" to "It's helpful for me to practice."

For additional assistance identifying and eliminating ANTs, head to my website for a workbook that you can share with your Creative: http://www.parentingtalent.com/ants-workbook-sign-up.

Learning to shift mindset around things that create fear and anxiety allows your Creative space to explore what positive outcomes may look like if they can set realistic goals within the learning process. For an artist who took a chance in submitting a work in a new-to-them medium, this may look like shifting the desired outcome from "I want to place in this competition" to "I want to learn as much as I can and have fun doing it, and I will give submission a try even though this is a new medium for me." If the goal can become the experience of creating art to submit, the outcome experience can be embraced as "even though I didn't place in the art competition, I learned a lot, I understand what I can work on, I met my goal of putting in work in a new medium, and I am making progress." This is very different from "I tried this new medium. I failed to place. I have no talent in this medium, so I should quit."

Helping your teen or tween Creative shift their mindset can be a very powerful tool. The benefits of a mindset shift tend to carry over into other areas of their lives as well. Once your Creative has mastered their ability to shift their mindset, they will find they have an easier time achieving their goals and finding success and happiness both within and outside of their art, even if the outcomes are not always exactly what they expected.

So how do we get them there? As parents, the first step is

modeling a growth mindset in our own lives, discussing what it was like to make the shift and the impact it has had on our experiences. Easier said than done, I know, but it truly is one of the most effective things we can do to create lasting positive changes in all of our lives.

When you embrace a growth mindset, share it with your Creative. They may give you the patented teen or tween eye roll, but they will hear you, and they will see you learning and growing as a result of your belief that change is possible. Some examples of embracing and modeling a growth mindset might include:

• "So I totally failed at making those cookies you asked me to make, but at least I learned a few things for the next time I try to bake them."

• "I thought I would never be a runner, but I tried a new program and got better shoes, and I'm actually moving along at a slow jog now—progress!"

• "Even though I'm frustrated that my new boss changed the entire workflow, I'm going to figure out how to make it work for me."

• "I used to think I could never learn how to set up my own website, but now that I've given myself a lot of time to learn and got okay with making a lot of mistakes, I've gotten pretty good at it."

Some suggestions to help encourage your teen or tween Creative to make this shift:

• Move away from focusing on big changes and instead look for minor adjustments or improvements you can use to measure progress. In the beginning, these should be small and very manageable.

• Remind them to shift away from thinking "I didn't" or "I can't" and instead start thinking "Not yet."

• Remind them to think back to a skill they thought they could never achieve but ultimately mastered.

• Encourage them to acknowledge their ANTs and address and challenge those thoughts. Sometimes, it helps to suggest that they think about what they would say to a friend who voiced the same negative self-talk out loud.

• If they are struggling, gently encourage them to consider whether they have a fixed mindset and have them ask themselves, "If I did have a growth mindset about this, what would that sound like?"

Chapter 6

Failure, Limiting Beliefs, and Accountability

It's hard, so hard, when you have wisdom and experience and can see a fall coming for your kid and can't stop it. M is so much like me—which honestly isn't great. I tend to procrastinate and only motivate myself when I'm up against a deadline. But my career lends itself to that in some ways.

M's goal is to be a TV news reporter. She is so fortunate to live in a suburban area where the high school has classes that help her work toward this goal. She desperately wanted to be an anchor for the school's in-house news show, but it was super competitive. She knew other kids were doing things to raise their profiles, volunteering as studio staff, hanging around for the open production meetings. And she'd say she was going to do those things, but then something would come up—an invitation to hang out after school, a quick shopping trip. I asked her if the other kids were practicing for their auditions, and she said, "Yeah, probably, Mom, but I don't really need to. I did really well in the class and they all know what I can do." I knew she was shooting herself in the foot, but I also knew that I kept rescuing her and that at some point she was just going to have to learn a hard lesson.

Well, as expected, when it came time for auditions, she did well, but she wasn't ultimately chosen. She was devastated—and at first a little indignant, claiming that one of the girls hadn't been as polished as she was. So I suggested she go get some feedback before the next round of auditions the following spring. For once she listened to me, and she went and spoke to the teacher, who told her she was great at on-camera banter, great at last-minute changes, but that that was the only thing she'd shown them, not being a team player and helping out around the studio, not trying to learn more by sitting in on production meetings when she didn't have to, and not showing everyone that she really wanted to get better by signing up for practice times on the teleprompter.

As sad as she was, M finally learned a lesson from her choices. She made a point of doing everything the teacher suggested for the entire semester. I'm proud to say that that was the only time she wasn't chosen for some type of on-camera position, and two years later, her teacher wrote her an amazing college recommendation letter that included "able to receive and implement feedback." If she makes it, she'll be great when she's up against a breaking news deadline, and she also gets that she can't rely only on that skill.

We live in an era where teens and tweens are expected to participate—and excel—in multiple areas. For us parents, it can be extremely challenging to see our kids struggling, or worse, not trying at all, and we may want to jump in and help out. This comes from a place of love. We don't want to see our kids struggle later, to regret not living up to their potential or mastering a skill that will be important later in life. We want to see our kids have strong work ethics and set themselves up for success. So the temptation becomes to nudge (*ahem, shove*) them back on track when they seem to be getting distracted or losing their way, to help them in any way we can, including sending reminders, making schedules, and, yes, running in to rescue them when they are in danger of making mistakes.

The irony of this is that, even though we're doing this because we're trying to raise independent, self-motivated, hard-working people, the result is often the exact opposite.

FAILURE

Failure is an important and necessary part of emotional growth. It is also inevitable. We learn from failure. It is part of taking chances, of exploring, of finding what works (and what does not). It's often necessary to fail in order to gain positive results and learn how to recover from mistakes. So, as scary as it is, it's best that, as parents, we encourage our children to occasionally engage in situations where failure is an almost guaranteed outcome and perfectionism is discouraged. The deepest lessons can come from failure, which teaches Creatives what not to do and how to make and own their own independent decisions.

Research has shown that children who have been protected from failure or have not been encouraged to fail are less excited about learning new things, less motivated to work hard, and overall less successful than children who have been allowed to make their own mistakes and miscalculations and face their own setbacks.[1] If you can help your Creative understand that failure is one of the best ways to improve and learn, you will be setting them up to have a more positive relationship with their art—and with all other endeavors down the line.

As your tween moves into their teen years, encourage

them to look up stories of the paths their creative heroes took to find success with their art. They would be hard-pressed to find anyone who has pursued creativity on either a recreational or professional level who does not have many stories of failures on their journey.

Another important outcome of learning to risk failure is that it counteracts self-limiting beliefs. When we repeatedly risk failure, it becomes evident that, even when we believe we will fail at something, there will also be times where we will succeed. This creates a real-life experience of nothing ventured, nothing gained.[2]

LIMITING BELIEFS

Self-limiting beliefs are the thoughts, opinions, or convictions we see as absolute thresholds that hold us back in some way. In the outstanding book *The Big Leap*, Dr. Gay Hendricks talks about how our self-limiting beliefs can keep us from hitting our highest potential. Hendricks proposes the concept of an "upper limit problem." He discusses how, in his work with hundreds of successful, driven, capable high-level executives, he noticed over time that many would sabotage themselves in reaching their highest potential. They would have a comfort zone, a level they believed was in their "zone of excellence," and, once that was reached, any achievement above it would lead to great anxiety—and self-sabotage. Hendricks identifies the highest level of achievement to be the "zone of genius" and says we have unconscious barriers that keep us from comfortably moving into the top level of what we are capable of. We create obstacles that don't really exist in order to stop progress.[3]

Hendricks identified four fears that act as barriers that keep us stuck—especially when things are going well. These barriers are:

1. Fear that we are undeserving of great success and happiness,
2. Fear of leaving people behind or being disloyal,
3. Fear that success will lead to bigger issues and problems or create bigger burdens to others, and
4. Fear of outshining others, making those around us look or feel bad.

Although your teen or tween may experience various shades and degrees of all four, a frequently occurring concern for young Creatives is the last: fear of outshining others. Teens and tweens often receive a societal message from their peers that if they shine too much, their success may be interpreted as bragging, showing off, or intentionally trying to make others look bad. Given that teens are so driven to pursue the acceptance of their peers, it can become a challenging struggle for them to produce at their best level—especially in a public forum—if they fear that doing so will put that acceptance at risk. There is fear of being disliked, targeted, torn down, or seen as arrogant if they work to achieve at their highest potential.

This can occur even in supportive environments.

H has always kind of been a quirky outsider. It never really bothered her. I'm a single mom, and I used to feel really bad about how much I was gone. H has always been attracted to an alternative aesthetic, and she started a YouTube channel as something to do when I wasn't home. I guess it kind of took off, and she really found her community, you know? So I was her biggest supporter and just ignored any of the parents who clearly thought I was crazy to let her do it. It's easy to say kids shouldn't do something if your kid fits in easily. But H also had tons of support from our extended family, and her contemporary music school she went to on weekends was super into [her alternative YouTube channel] too.

We had to move, and I felt horrible, but I just couldn't afford to stay in our old place. I was really worried H would have a hard time changing schools, but at first it seemed great. She found friends, and suddenly she was going out and doing things. I was really relieved and happy for her—but I noticed she was making videos and then not posting them. I asked her if something was wrong, but she said no.

I got worried because her channel had really been starting doing well, and it was weird for her to stop. I even asked to see one of the videos she had as unlisted, and it was fine—I guess I had been a little worried it was going to say she was depressed or something when I watched—but it was normal stuff, even talking about how great it was that she'd found a group who liked the same stuff she did.

I came home one night, and H was all hyped up. Another pretty big female alternative channel had reached out to see if she was okay since she'd stopped posting—it's amazing that they even noticed—and asked if she wanted to do a collaboration. I was super excited for her and asked what they were going to do. Then she got quiet and said she wasn't sure she was going to do it.

Then it all came out. She'd found friends who actually really felt like real friends, and they were all into alternative things in some way, and the leader of the group was really trying to get her own YouTube channel to take off. H said the girl was clearly jealous of her channel's following and would say things—less than complimentary things—about her videos, then try to say she was just joking. The other girls had all told her privately to ignore it, but she was the new girl in the group and she didn't want to cause problems, so she'd stopped posting and had told the group she wasn't sure if she was going to keep going.

But I could tell she really missed it—and this potential collaboration was a big deal. But H was worried that she'd hurt the leader girl's feelings or would be cut out of the group or something, and she was really torn. She knew it shouldn't stop her, but she really didn't want to seem like she was showing off. I was pretty frustrated, but I knew I had to let her decide. Thankfully, she was getting pretty close to another girl in the group, so H finally told her what was up, and that girl—love her—was excited and told her she had to do it. The friend kinda set the tone for the rest of the group, and even if she was faking it, the leader was supportive.

Now H tries to include her friends on her channel, but even that is complicated because one of the girls' parents doesn't want her on it, so while all the other girls want to be on the channel, H feels bad leaving anyone out. She really understands how bad that feels. And she still worries about being seen as showing off, so she downplays how well she's doing. It's hard to build an audience, and the collaboration helped her—she gained a lot of new followers. And sometimes it feels like she can't really enjoy it and she holds back from building on it.

Another way that young Creatives can be stuck by an upper limit problem is by buying into what some adults, including authority figures, may be telling them. Good, well-mannered, respectful kids listen to what adults—especially those who may be considered experts—have to say about their skills. They may not openly challenge authority, which, in turn, can mean not challenging negative, limiting comments.

A has been a talented artist from the time she was little. My husband's side of the family is artistic, so it makes sense. A used to love art—all forms, drawing, painting, clay work.

When she was really young, she was super advanced for her age. Lots of positive feedback, and adults were always surprised by her talent. But when she got a little older, she struggled a bit. A new art instructor tore her down, telling her she was average and lacked some basic skills that she needed to work on.

The best we could figure out was that [the instructor] was trying to motivate her not to rely on her talent and to dig into learning specific techniques, but all A heard was "average." She stopped believing she was capable of being great, and eventually she stopped trying.

I admit, I was so disappointed with both her and the instructor. But fast-forward, she did come back to art in high school, found her love for it again, and excelled.

Her bedroom is set up as a full art studio. Yet when she would tell people she was going to be an art major, so many said, "Oh, starving artist, huh?" or "Are you going to teach? How else can you make money?" This time, we knew how to handle it better, and we talked a lot about not letting others tell her what her probable outcomes were. We reminded her that she could be polite and tell them her plan—and she did have one—or she could just smile and shrug and know that the opinion of one person or someone who was not an artist shouldn't matter enough to bring her down.

It can be important for Creatives to be encouraged to be critical thinkers when it comes to feedback. It is very easy to use negative feedback as an excuse to "upper limit" ourselves and avoid pushing through to our full potential. Being able to remember that our current reality is not, and does not have to be, our forever reality is important, both for accepting and moving forward when failure occurs and for addressing less-than-constructive external feedback. Encourage your Creative to take a moment to process the feedback, decide what, if any, part of it is valuable information, let go of what is not useful, and make a plan to act on any parts that are valid.

This type of resistance to good things happening may be subtle. As your Creative finds success in their art, they may appear to be embracing the experience while, unconsciously, they are no longer doing their best. Sometimes, no matter how much enjoyment they derive from their art at times, their art may still be the easiest place for them to loosen the reins on accountability, whether that means neglecting it entirely or staying safe and only using the skills they have already mastered.

Other times, the resistance may be a more obvious failure outside of their art. They may be continuing to excel in their art, but, suddenly, their performance elsewhere may start to slide. For example, your straight-A student may find themselves the only freshman at their school to make it into their all-state choir. Up until they found out they had made it, their grades were fine, even though they had been juggling a very heavy load of choir practice, ensemble practice, school musical rehearsal, private lessons, and singing in their church choir. But, upon finding out they had made All-State, their grades may suddenly slip even though nothing obvious changed in their workload, confusing you as a parent. The student had managed to balance it all before they knew they had made it, but then, suddenly, after this amazing news, you see something change that may feel unrelated.

It's as if we tend to feel as though we can't possibly have too many things going well in our lives, so when things are going so well in some areas that it feels too good to be true, we unconsciously back away in other areas to compensate. Because this tends to be a very ingrained response for some, I've found it's often necessary to engage teens and tweens in conversations around accountability when addressing this type of behavior.

ACCOUNTABILITY

Learning to take personal accountability for our daily habits, our actions, our choices, and our mindset is central to avoiding self-sabotage. For teens and tweens, this is a developmental skill that is still in formation. They are learning a new level of accountability in so many areas of their lives: for schoolwork, studying, chores, other activities, and sometimes outside jobs, new love relationships, or a host of other developmentally appropriate tasks. It can be overwhelming.

With teens and tweens who are in the middle of learning how to juggle this increased accountability, internal accountability may be especially challenging at times. You may witness some serious self-sabotage when it comes to skill development. Sometimes adding some external accountability—and by that, I mean accountability to anyone other than you as a parent—can help stop self-sabotaging behaviors.

External accountability may be built in many ways. A common example is that, if your Creative's high school requires a minimum GPA to participate in certain activities that they are invested in, they may study to ensure they can participate. Another way to build external accountability is to connect your Creative to a larger group of their peers who are counting on them to come through on their end. This may be a formal group, like an ensemble, a group project, or a show, or an informal one, like a partnership with a fellow Creative to make sure work is getting done. There are all kinds of accountability or mastermind groups, formal or informal, that your Creative may buy into.

Another benefit of external accountability is that you tend to become a part of what you are around. If your Creative is surrounded by other artists who are passionate about the same things they are, who aim high, who encourage stepping outside of their comfort zone, and who care about and recognize progress, they are more likely to do the same.

When thinking about accountability, go back to the Four Tendencies framework and think about which category your Creative falls into. Knowing where they may struggle with holding themselves accountable—internally or externally—can assist you in finding ways to address accountability in a manner that works for their growth and development.

Failure is a part of growth, both within an art and as an individual. Let your Creative know you are proud of their effort and believe they are capable of whatever greatness they set their mind to, and hold them accountable for reaching for their goals even when it seems challenging. If you see them coming up against an upper limit problem, help them identify what is holding them back and find ways to push through.

Chapter 7

Negativity Bias, Vulnerability, Shame, and Resilience

I love my kid—but she is so negative. Here's an example: she scored all nines or tens out of tens in her cello competition. She was amazing, and her teacher was thrilled. But what did she focus on? She had almost tripped walking out onto the stage [before performing]. She had caught herself, it was fine, and, yes, one of the judges had asked if she was okay and if she needed a minute—because, gee, being considerate? Trying to set her up for success? Nope. In her head, she heard something like "Clearly you are a klutz and need some time to steady yourself. How could a klutz like you play cello well?"

If you ask her how the competition was, she'll say, "It was awful, I totally embarrassed myself." No mention of "Oh gee, and I got the highest scores of all of the students in my studio," or "I hit a new personal best."

NEGATIVITY BIAS

Why is it so easy to not only remember negative events but also dwell on them indefinitely? In chapter 5, I discussed those pesky ANTs—automatic negative thoughts—as well as our tendency to have repetitive thoughts. In addition to our proclivity to automatically create negative scenarios that pop into our heads uninvited, we humans are also wired with a negativity bias that not only keeps us noticing external negative information or experiences but highlights those negatives in our memory.[1]

Negativity bias causes us to pay attention to, learn from, and use negative information more readily than positive input.[2] Again, from an evolutionary standpoint, this makes sense. Unfortunately, most people can pull up examples from their own modern life. Even if your boss sings your praises at your review, it can be hard to recall all of what they said—but most of us can remember with perfect clarity the list of "room for improvement" items tacked on at the end.

This is also the reason we remember insults over praise, and, when presented with equally negative and positive events, we tend to respond more intensely to the negative ones. This is true both emotionally and physically. It is also part of the reason why we recall traumatic events more easily than positive ones.

If that isn't bad enough, research also suggests that we tend to believe negative feedback more readily than positive feedback.[3] As we take in more negative information, the weight of that information is seen as more valid.

Wondering why this is? Back to those evolutionary traits that were once helpful but are now a hindrance. Recalling the exact shape of the leaves of a berry that made you violently ill is more important to survival than recalling the same for all of the other berries around. The more prehistoric people could attend to negative stimuli, the more likely they were to survive and go on to procreate.

For Creatives, this means they may remember the times they messed up, didn't win, failed to progress, or had any other less-than-ideal outcome related to their art more readily than they remember the times they won, made huge progress, received standing ovations, or met with outcomes that far exceeded their expectations. Their ANTs are fueled by brains that filter out positive experiences related to their art to put more emphasis on "poisoned" experiences than pleasurable ones.

VULNERABILITY AND SHAME

You know that feeling in the pit of your stomach when you take a chance and step out of your comfort zone and risk losing control of an outcome? That's vulnerability. We all struggle with some degree of emotional vulnerability to varying extents during our daily lives, but Creatives often experience this repeatedly as they share their art, something very personal to them, with the world.

Vulnerability requires one to be fully present and share their authentic self without defensiveness, understanding that there is a risk of being negatively received or judged. When a Creative is sharing what they love, what they created, what is often part of the core of their identity, they are stepping into vulnerability.

Thanks to the work of Dr. Brené Brown, the concept of emotional vulnerability gained widespread acknowledgment, especially after her now-famous TED talk, "Listening to Shame." If you have not watched it, I suggest you and your Creative both take twenty minutes and do so. Vulnerability, according to Brown, is "uncertainty, risk, and emotional exposure."[4] Brown also says vulnerability is necessary for creativity, stating in her book *Daring Greatly* that "Vulnerability is the birthplace of love, belonging, joy, courage, empathy, and creativity."[5] Creativity allows the fullness of who one is to be shared, yet this must be done in an unpredictable world where rejection, the unknown, and competition are part of life. Showing up and taking risks can provoke deep fear. Potential rejection is inevitable when taking risks, but feeling rejected can lead to feelings of shame.

Brown describes shame as an "intensely painful feeling or experience of believing that we are flawed and therefore unworthy of love and belonging."[6] Feelings of shame can come from being shamed externally or from feeling internally ashamed. Rejection, public scrutiny, or devaluation can arise when one is perceived to be deviating from social norms or from what is expected or when one simply makes a mistake. For teen or tween Creatives, these outcomes may look like harsh criticism, being laughed at, or being teased for their efforts.

> K is super funny. She started out as an actor, but as part of her training, she had to learn improv. From there, she realized she loves comedy, especially stand-up comedy. She started doing small bits on her TikTok account, and she started getting not just likes but actual followers and fans and lots of nice comments. But we also have to watch [the comments] really carefully. She will get over a hundred positive comments and then one troll will come on and say something negative. It's crazy because they attack her on a personal level. One guy commented something like "keep trying to be funny when you are that ugly and maybe someday you'll make a guy laugh at something besides your face." K is attractive, and lots of commenters after that called the guy out, but what does K focus on? His horrible comment. She knows that he's just a troll and that it comes

with the territory, but it's like she can't forget the negative comments, and sometimes she'll start to spiral into a space of trying to get the trolls to like her. We must watch how it's affecting her, and we've told her we will force her to take a break if it's impacting her happiness.

Shame can become part of self-identity, which, in turn, may turn into creative paralysis. Feeling one is unworthy, unlovable, and incapable undermines a sense of self-worth. It can feel safer to avoid creative output or avoid *sharing* creative output. If one stifles expression of authentic feelings or effort, then there is an artificial protection from judgment.

In this era where social media is an integral part of society, the opportunities for both vulnerability and shame are constant. For the young Creative, there may be very real fear and anxiety about being vulnerable, especially with social media often keeping shame triggers alive and available in a public forum for a Creative's peers to see. Most teens and tweens have experienced shame and embarrassment connected to social media or a social interaction at some point, which then feeds into a negativity bias around being vulnerable—and a quelling of creative expression and exploration.

I was feeling really sad for M and wasn't sure how to help him. He was always kind of larger-than-life—he'd ask all the questions, he'd volunteer to try things, he was always up for something new, and he was always playing his guitar for everyone. That was, until sleepaway camp two years ago.

Some young, inexperienced, and clearly under-trained high school counselors set up a water balloon version of dodgeball on a hot day. M was having fun until he saw the counselors laughing on the side. M is many things, but coordinated is not one of them. Many of the other boys had been playing baseball for years at that point, but M never had an interest, so he never became really good at throwing—especially overhand with aim. He was laughing and having fun even though he was getting nailed with balloons, but the counselors were laughing at how he threw the balloons. Afterwards, they said something like "Okay, some of you need help," and they called M and another boy up to "teach" them to throw properly. This led the other boys, who hadn't been focusing on M's throwing, to snicker and yell out tips.

M was humiliated. The camp apologized, but that will never make up for what that situation did to him. Now he's scared to put himself out there. I didn't even realize that that's what had happened until his guitar teacher offered to let him sit in on a gig he had, which he'd done before. M declined, and, when I pushed him about why, he said he was scared because he wasn't as good as the professionals and he didn't want to humiliate himself because this time he at least knew he wasn't good—not like the water balloon thing at camp.

If your Creative can learn to articulate feelings of shame, they are less likely to hold on to those feelings. When they can put those feelings into words, they will be better able to identify the emotions that led to the feelings of shame, which can then lead to better counteracting that shame. This is hard, as it is a very vulnerable thing to do. Yet if we recognize that we all feel shame at times, and if we can identify these emotions and then take a step outside of it and look at what is happening to us in the moment, we may be able to stop—or at least lessen—those emotions.

Going back to the example above, a critical point that M shared later was that the night before the water balloon incident, the same counselors who were laughing at him had been "humiliated" by some girls from their sister camp.

Armed with this information, we worked through looking at the situation as outside observers, and M was able to understand that the boys' actions likely had little to do with his throwing ability but rather with their own immature coping strategies. He realized they were trying to make someone else feel shame instead of managing their own emotions. He was finally able to move on and get back to performing, starting small in a very safe environment.

RESILIENCE

Resilience is defined as "the process of adapting well in the face of adversity, trauma, tragedy, threats, or even significant sources of stress."[7] We tend to think of it as the ability to bounce back from a negative experience. When we see someone bend but not break under the weight of a challenge, an emotional wound, or a setback, we tend to think of them as resilient.

Cultivating emotional resilience should be part of the growth and development of young artists. In order for a Creative to explore, advance, and expand on new skills, their ability to be open, connected, and vulnerable must be nurtured, encouraged, and supported. Acknowledging and connecting to emotion, and being willing to be vulnerable and learn from those moments, is how resilience is nurtured. Creatives have to learn to be resilient when things don't turn out the way they expect them to. Living creatively requires the ability to function in a state of trial and error—of making mistakes.

Resilience for teens can be a challenge. They are in a stage that often includes struggling with self-identity and competence. Yet achieving a certain amount of resilience is a fundamental step on the path to adulthood, when life will become increasingly complicated. It is natural and normal to have uncomfortable feelings after a negative event, but learning to respond in healthy ways is important for your teen's ability to pick themselves back up after adversity.

A teen or tween Creative's art may create situations that are challenging and require resilience to navigate. Teens and tweens are generally rewarded for fitting in, not standing out. The very act of doing something outside their peers' perceived social norms is hard. If your Creative's art is something others around them don't understand or appreciate, or is considered "showing off," then your Creative may have ample opportunity to practice resilience. Practicing their art, especially in public, may be emotionally challenging when they are developmentally in an environment where their peers can be brutal and competitive.

In addition, the learning process for creative skills requires showing up, being present, being open to feedback and criticism, and having self-compassion. Even many adults have a hard time engaging in these behaviors, and we may be asking our Creative teens and tweens to do these things on a regular basis. Be aware of how hard this is and recognize the vulnerability it takes, and notice and praise your Creative's resilience when you see them working their way through challenging moments.

Believing the outcome one desires is possible is challenging when you are coming from a place of negativity bias. Combine that with having to be vulnerable and avoiding feelings of shame, and it can be hard for a Creative to engage in both enjoying and growing in their art. Knowing your Creative also has to be vulnerable and avoid feelings of shame, it can be hard to support and encourage them to engage in both enjoying and growing in their art. There may be moments where they have meltdowns, throw angry fits, or threaten to quit. It's important to remember this is temporary and they can process and work through it, finding resilience when they feel safe again after the moment has passed.

Here are a few things that can help encourage the Creative in your world to step into vulnerability.

• **Seek out or create a safe environment.** Encourage your Creative to create or share art in places that feel safe from irrelevant negativity. Avoid sharing online, or disable comments if they cause emotional negativity.

• **Offer validation.** Acknowledge and validate hard things. "This is hard. You are brave for trying this."

• **Seek out and create environments within the art that provide validation and social connection with peers of a similar age.** This can be in real life or in a virtual group. Find a place where peers are supportive and are genuinely excited by what is being created and shared.

• **Set short-term goals.** Rather than focusing on something that may take months or even years to master, set a goal that can be accomplished in one or two weeks—and celebrate when the goal is met.

• **Set goals with easily attainable and measurable success.** Instead of "I'm going to put together this entire video in one week," have your Creative start with a manageable, measurable goal, such as "Today I'm going to upload all of the videos by the end of the day. Tomorrow, I will sort the videos into categories." (Other Creatives might set a goal of sorting half of the videos, or even fewer.)

• **Protect unstructured time within the art.** Encourage your Creative to find time to just have fun, to go over skills that are mastered, to "play" with their art. Often, it's during these times that the structured, learned skills click and a breakthrough is made.

• **Celebrate effort.** When the Creative shows up, has worked to be prepared, and gives their best effort, celebrate the effort —and focus less on the outcome.

Part II

Navigating the
Obstacles in Your
Creative's Life

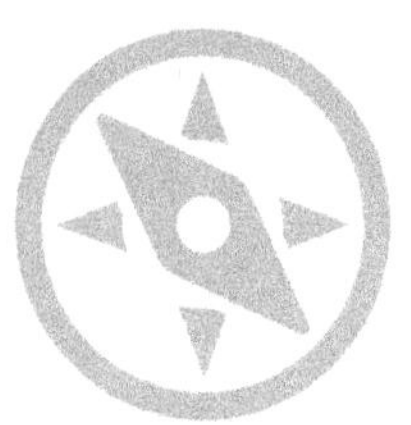

Chapter 8
Mental Health Concerns

In addition to the struggles that come with navigating their art, Creatives also have to deal with the same challenges and struggles as their peers. Peer pressure, occasional sadness, overwhelm, academic pressure, breakups, shame, and social anxieties are all part of the teen and tween experience. The emotional sensitivity, connectedness to others and their environment, and increased perceptiveness that some Creatives possess may intensify their emotional experience of certain situations.

Add to this the challenges inherent to being a Creative, including potential frequent rejections (such as those that come with auditioning, submitting art, or submitting writing), performance anxiety, finding balance between artistic wants and needs and the demands of school, and vulnerability when it's time to share their art openly... and extra support in the form of psychotherapy may be beneficial.

If your Creative expresses a desire or need for psychotherapy, that should not be cause for alarm. In fact, by seeking help, your Creative may open up new levels of creativity and vulnerability (and the ability to tolerate that vulnerability effectively), feel empowered, and develop new coping skills. Psychotherapy can aid them in setting healthy boundaries, increase their communication skills, and assist them in making better choices connected to their art.

Some Creatives do express a unique conflict when deciding whether they should engage in therapy. The fear that, by engaging in therapy, the very core of what makes them "creative" may be "normalized" and thus they may lose their creativity is one that may keep some Creatives from seeking support or intervention. The irony of this thought process is that when one *doesn't* seek help, creativity is often negatively impacted by the deterioration of mental health. Unhealthy potential maladaptive coping mechanisms, such as substance abuse, only serve to have a further negative impact on creativity. So, if you feel your Creative would benefit from therapy but they are resistant, see if you can get to the root of the issue, including asking if they feel therapy might "change" them in a way that doesn't fit with their self-concept.

With all of the emotional upheavals that can arise during typical teen and tween development, distinguishing normal teen behavior, emotional disruptions, and outbursts from serious problems can be a huge challenge. Part of being a parent is working to allow the independence and growth that are natural and necessary parts of growing up while also being available to your Creative when they need help.

I wish I'd known sooner. Everyone—including us—was so into what B was doing that they dismissed the signs that something was wrong. And I feel so bad about that. But because his grades were still okay, we were happy to believe that he was just super dedicated to his craft and that that was why it was all he would talk about, why he stopped spending time with his friends, why he was staying up so late working. At first, we were actually happy because we thought it was just a great work ethic. We didn't notice when it went from healthy to unhealthy until it all fell apart.

Often, mental health concerns, stress, negative emotional well-being, and relationship challenges start in a manner that feels manageable. First breakups, hard classes, changing friendships, increased expectations, and increased competition are all expected challenges and hurdles during middle and high school. Creatives are often highly sensitive people. They are sensitive to the feelings of others, and they tend to be in touch with their own feelings. They care very deeply about the people and world around them, how they are perceived, how they present to others, and if they are meeting the needs of others.

Combine this with normal teen and tween hypersensitivity and hyper-self-awareness, and Creatives have an increased potential to become vulnerable to mental health issues. Fifty percent of serious mental illness begins by age fourteen. Seventy-five percent begins by age twenty-four.[1] For parents, those statistics can be very scary to see.

My first advice when advising parents is to trust your gut. If you find yourself googling "When is depression a problem?" then you are sensing something isn't right. You are an expert on your child, but you are most likely not an expert on mental health. Even if you are a licensed therapist, you cannot be objective about your own child. If you are wondering if there may be a chance that expert assessment or intervention is needed, always err on the side of getting a professional opinion or diagnosis. Even if the professional determines that there is no immediate need for intervention, you will have someone to check in with if things escalate, and, if your teen is open to it, they will have an outlet to work through the concerns that led you to reach out in the first place.

Detecting mental health concerns in a teen or tween can be challenging. While awareness of mental health issues is increasing, there continue to be underlying stereotypes about various types of mental health disorders. Society continues to portray those with depression as people who sleep all day and keep their blinds down. We don't necessarily make the same connection when a person suddenly becomes very irritable, is no longer sleeping much, has escalating conflicts with friends and family, and suddenly decides they are no longer interested in their art—but all of these may be indicative of underlying clinical depression in a teen or tween.

As parents, we are all striving to have the best, most open relationships with our teens or tweens that we can manage. This can be a challenge and requires quite a bit of work. Your Creative will not suddenly open up and share if something is wrong unless you have a history of safe and validating past communication. Some suggestions for establishing and maintaining this type of communication include:

• **Create a safe place for them to communicate.** Offer to drive them to activities, take them out for a special treat, or look for any other way you can carve out time alone with them. Do not have an agenda or try to force a conversation to obtain more information. If they learn that you are available, then, if and when they need to share, they will be more likely to do so.

• **Accept *how* your teen or tween communicates.** If this is via text, don't force a face-to-face conversation. You may ask for one, but if they pull back or refuse, respect their need to have some space when sharing.

• **Accept *when* they communicate.** Yes, it's often very likely to be at a less-than-ideal time for you, but unless you are in the middle of an activity that simply cannot be interrupted, try to stop and listen. My fellow teen parents and I joke that the best way to find out what is going on in your teen or tween's world is to plan to go to bed early and get a good night's rest—that always seems to be when suddenly your teen texts asking if you can talk.

• **Listen.** It sounds easy, but it can be very hard. When your teen or tween opens up, you may feel pressure to try to cram in all of the concerns, advice, and general opinions you have been holding back. Don't do it. Just listen. If they ask for feedback, this is not the time for some intense lecture series on choices, actions, or decisions. Your reactions matter; your teen or tween will sense if you are waiting to pounce and offer up advice. There will be time for that later, but for now, it's fine to say, "Wow, you have a lot going on. Is it okay for me to circle back to some of this later on?"

This may seem obvious to many; however, it's critical to creating a relationship based on trust and openness, which is what is needed for a teen or tween to find the courage to share with you when they are struggling.

If you find yourself worried that your Creative is becoming overwhelmed or is struggling emotionally, here are some things to consider.

• How is your Creative doing in school?

• Have there been any noticeable changes in their grades?

• How are they doing socially?

• Do they feel good about the number of friends they have in their lives?

• If they desire community, do they have one?

• Have you noticed any other behavior changes, such as changes in eating habits or sleep habits or inappropriate or disproportionate emotional reactions, increased irritability, or outbursts of anger? How about increased sadness or any sudden disinterest in activities they previously enjoyed?

These are all signs that there may be a more serious issue occurring than just "teenage moodiness" (especially if more than one of these signs is present). These signs indicate that a professional opinion is likely needed.

If you notice any of the following, immediate professional therapeutic intervention and assessment is indicated:

• Participation in illegal activities

• Acting out sexually

• Self-harm, including cutting

• Abusing substances

• Running away or disappearing for periods of time where you cannot reach them

• Thoughts of suicide or making a suicide plan or attempt

If, for any reason, you suspect or sense that your Creative is dealing with an urgent, potentially life-threatening emergency mental health crisis, call emergency services or take them to your nearest emergency room.

Below are lists of symptoms for some of the more common mental health disorders. These are only some examples of when mental health concerns warrant more attention (and potentially professional care).

As you read, keep in mind that mental health is a complex and nuanced concern. Each one of the disorders listed below has a multitude of books dedicated to researching it, identifying it, explaining it, and advising how to navigate it. This list is in no way comprehensive, and it is not intended for diagnosis in any capacity. Only a health professional who has met with and assessed your teen or tween is qualified to make any diagnosis. This is simply offered as one starting point to help you consider if some behaviors you have seen in your Creative (or behaviors they self-report) may be yellow or red flags.

ANXIETY

Teens and tweens with anxiety may:

• Have difficulty concentrating,

• Report jumpiness or being on edge,

• Experience a constant state of dread,

• Focus on negative outcomes,

• Demonstrate recurring feelings of worry and stress about everyday activities, relationships, and events,

• Experience unexplained stomachaches or headaches,

• Report sweating, shaking, or feeling nauseous—especially in social situations,

• Experience panic attacks, or

• Report a loss of appetite or no longer enjoying favorite foods.

> T was, like so many of us, totally lost during the lockdown. She had always had a group of friends, but she felt like she had to work to keep them—like, they liked her and were happy to include her, but to her it kind of felt like an afterthought, an "Oh yeah, add T to this group text about plans" kind of thing. So during the early days of the pandemic, when she couldn't see anyone, she felt really isolated.
>
> She'd always had some anxiety, but she'd figured out how to manage it. Well, we quickly began to notice her anxiety was getting worse. She started having what I now know are panic attacks—especially around her watercolors. If she couldn't get something right almost right away, she'd get super upset, like disproportionally upset. She was super irritable on the days when she had her online art class and hated doing [the class] remotely. Then she started really freaking out the day before her lessons, wanting to redo her paintings, even wanting to skip her school classes to paint. Finally one day, when I told her no, that she had to go to class and paint after her academic day was over, she lost it. She was crying—sobbing, really—and she couldn't breathe. It was like she couldn't hear us trying to calm her down. Then she said her chest was hurting. We took her to the ER and that's where we learned she was having a panic attack.

DEPRESSION

Teens and tweens with depression may:

• Have insomnia or start sleeping more than normal,

• Engage in social isolation,

• Report tiredness or loss of energy,

• Show increased irritability, agitation, or restlessness,

• Show decreased concern with personal hygiene or appearance,

• Have changes in appetite, either decreased interest in food (potentially leading to weight loss) or increased cravings for food (potentially leading to weight gain),

• Have angry outbursts atypical for them,

• Engage in risky or disruptive behavior,

• Report unexplained headaches or body aches that don't respond to over-the-counter medication, and

• Begin visiting the school nurse more frequently.

> N was always a kind of moody kid. He'd come back from camping trips with the cousins and, while all the other kids would be talking about how much fun they had had, N would usually just shrug and say that the trip was fine. He has always preferred his own company, so we didn't think much about it when he stopped going out with his friends on

the weekends and would just stay in his room writing music. I did notice he was gaining some weight, but I didn't want to say anything and make him feel bad about his appearance.

It wasn't until he got into a fight with his little sister that I got worried. Before then, he had been her biggest fan, but all of a sudden everything she did annoyed him. He was either being mean or hurtful—when he'd bother speaking to her, that is. His music instructor commented that he seemed to not be coming as prepared as he usually did and that he wasn't asking a lot of questions, which was not like him at all.

I took him in for a doctor's appointment, just to make sure everything was okay. I thought maybe he needed a supplement or something, but luckily they did a mental health screening in his intake and he scored off the chart for depression. He reported things I hadn't noticed, which made me feel horrible, but I was glad the doctor gave him a referral to a therapist and the therapist helped him start medication.

ATTENTION DEFICIT HYPERACTIVITY DISORDER

Teens and tweens with ADHD may:

• Be easily distracted or show poor attention spans,

• Be forgetful or often lose/misplace things,

• Be unable to complete tasks that are tedious, boring, or time-consuming,

• Have difficulty organizing tasks or assignments,

• Be unable to concentrate on tasks even when they want to,

- Interrupt conversations,

- Have little or no sense of physical danger,

- Act without thinking about the consequences,

- Constantly change from one activity to another or have difficulty changing from one activity to another, and

- Have an inability to carry out multistep instructions.

A has always been a high-energy kid, but no one ever described her as hyperactive. She could sit still when she had to. But she is happiest when she is moving. We got her into dance early. She thrived. She's super smart, but her grades were always just okay. She loved elementary school—she went to a program where there was a lot of group learning, a lot of movement, and learning by doing. Middle school wasn't as smooth, but by then she was doing a lot of regional theater and we'd have to pull her out of school, so we just thought it was that. And she'd always do her work—in fact, she preferred when she was in a show because she had to do a lot of her work outside of school and could do her assignments standing up or in some other crazy position. Again, we just attributed that to her previous school, which didn't care how they got work done as long as it wasn't bothering anyone.

But then high school started, and the wheels came off the bus. A's grades tanked. She nearly failed science, which was her last class of the day. She said she tried but just couldn't concentrate there. She lost three sets of house keys. Her dad was so mad that he installed a keypad lock at his place. She'd sleep at my place, forget her sheet music, and not realize it until the next morning at her dad's.

Her dad was pretty angry and threatened to take her out of acting. He felt like if she could memorize pages of dialogue, she could memorize her geometry proofs. [As he told her this] she was crying, saying that she did want to do well in school but she just couldn't make herself do things that were boring. Her dad said that that just proved she was being lazy.

It was her dad's brother, her uncle, who said something to her dad after A spent some time with his kids at their family cabin. He had been diagnosed with ADHD as an adult, and he said watching A was like watching himself at that age. He urged my husband to talk to me and get her evaluated—he said he'd wished he'd known at that age, that his life would have been easier. So this summer we had her evaluated and she started some medication, and her counselor gave her some tips and tricks for staying on top of things.

She's so much happier—and I wouldn't have described her as unhappy. But she said, "It's like someone turned down the noise in my head so I can focus on things even when they aren't that interesting."

AUTISM SPECTRUM DISORDER

Teens and tweens with ASD may:

• Talk about a favorite topic but have a hard time talking about or listening to others talk about other subjects,

• Have above-average vocabulary but speak in a more formal manner than their peers,

• Take language very literally,

• Have trouble taking turns in conversations,

• Find it challenging to follow more than three steps at a time, especially for things they are not interested in doing,

• Have trouble interpreting nonverbal cues such as tone of voice or body language,

• Use eye contact less than others or avoid eye contact when they are being spoken to,

• Prefer to spend time alone or with people older than themselves,

• Have trouble understanding the unspoken rules of friendships,

• Have trouble understanding personal space and get too close to people,

• Be very sensitive to certain sensory stimuli or experiences,

• Seek certain sensory stimuli or experiences, and

• Have difficulty going to sleep or staying asleep.

> P got into photography as a young boy. People always described him as a quirky kid. On our walks, he paid attention to detail, noticing things I'd never see, and wanted my phone to take pictures of things he saw. He'd get frustrated by how poor the quality was, so I started letting him use my digital camera—and he'd wind up taking better nature pictures than me.
>
> His grandparents gave him his first DSLR camera when he was eleven. He liked being known as "the kid who takes pictures," preferring to observe action rather than being a

part of it. He always had friends, though now, looking back, he'd cycle through them every two years or so and then they'd seem to drift away. But because he was invited to parties and some playdates, we didn't notice anything unusual until middle school.

My husband and I are both introverts, so we chalked up the decrease in social interaction to the changes in middle school—larger parties, more strangers, just not P's thing. This was also when his photography hit a new level. The only thing he wanted for his birthday was Adobe Photoshop, so we gave him that. He'd spend hours editing photos. We'd have to remind him to go to bed. When we'd say, "You need to get out a little more" or "You should try to hang out with your friends," he'd say, "Why? I'm weird. I like working on this stuff and not all that stupid stuff everyone talks about at school."

By high school, he was a loner. But I could tell, when I pushed him, that he didn't want to be alone, but he was having trouble making friends. He couldn't take a photography class right away at school, but with some insistence on our part, he did join the after-school photography club and applied to be a freelance photographer for his school newspaper and yearbook. He found a welcoming peer group there.

One day, I was dropping off a snack at his photography club and I heard him critiquing one of his friends' photos. He was being brutal, and I peeked in and could see that his friend looked upset. I said something to P later, and he looked at me like I was crazy and said, "He said to tell him the truth." He truly did not see how hurtful his tone and choice of words might feel.

Freshman year of college was when it all clicked. He had a professor who had ASD and openly shared this with his students, in part to help them understand some of his atypical behaviors and communication. In a conversation after class, the professor implied that my son understood something that had happened in class because he had the same diagnosis as the professor. My son had no idea what he was talking about, but he looked it up and called me, saying, "Mom, I finally know what's wrong with me."

I was confused because we never experienced him as having something "wrong" with him, but it turns out that that was how he experienced himself—as having something wrong inside of him. He made himself an appointment with campus counseling and took several tests, and it turned out he was right. It's funny, had we known, it probably wouldn't have changed much for him—he did okay. But it would have probably changed some stuff for me and how I dealt with things. Like the time he begged to go to photography camp, but then begged to come home one day after camp started and I forced him to stay. Now I realize that all of his complaints—that the sheets were scratchy to him, the food was different, the lights in the cabin were too bright—were all legitimate sensory triggers for him and he was truly miserable. But I'm so grateful for his photography. It really helps him stay involved with others, but in a way that works for him.

BIPOLAR DISORDER

Teens and tweens with bipolar disorder may:

- Have periods of appearing euphoric or immature,

- Be short-tempered,

- Have trouble focusing on tasks,

- Participate in high-risk activities,

- Show heightened interest in sex or sexual talk,

- Speak quickly,

- Move from subject to subject in a conversation,

- Express periods of extreme sadness,

- Report frequent headaches, stomachaches, or bodily pain,

- Over- or under-eat,

- Have insomnia or start sleeping more than normal,

- Have significant mood swings, and

- Not respond well to antidepressant therapy.

We first noticed something was going on with T when we moved to Chicago from Florida. She'd always been kind of a moody kid and now she was withdrawn and sad, but we figured it was due to the move. She had left her friends and, with it being her freshman year, we knew the timing was really bad for her. We'd never planned to relocate, so we were all struggling with the change and trying to make the best of it. We'd promised her new equipment for her YouTube channel to try to lift her spirits.

She'd gotten into a fight with her friend group right before we moved—my therapist at the time thought maybe it was her way of protecting herself, sabotaging the friendships so she wouldn't miss them. It made sense to me. She did make some new friends at school, and she'd seem happy at times, but when she was home, she was either working on her YouTube channel or sleeping.

When winter hit, it got much worse. She stopped going out, would miss school saying she didn't feel well, and barely showered unless we insisted. She stopped posting videos on YouTube—which was surprising to us because she'd worked really hard to get over one thousand subscribers. We had to force her to come downstairs on Christmas morning, and she could barely manage a thank you for the expensive camera her grandparents gave her.

I called her doctor, and they fit her in over winter break and started her on antidepressants. My husband and I were hopeful this would change things, but they continued to get worse. She'd bite our heads off just for asking her if she wanted dinner. We finally insisted she go to therapy when she was in danger of failing several classes. She agreed only because it was the only way to get the school to work with us to keep her from failing.

Initially, her therapist diagnosed her with depression, but, like us, was saying she had gone through a significant loss recently and it might be a situational reaction. Then, sometime in March, we noticed a change in her. She seemed to be getting better and was more energized. In late March, T came bounding down the stairs, showered, dressed, and vlogging. I'd thought I'd heard her stirring around during the night and had been worried about getting her up and out the door for school, but here she was ready to go.

When I asked what had changed and she flippantly said, "Well, all the drugs and therapy are working, I guess," I remember my husband said, "So, who turned her back on?" She said she wanted to walk to school so she could vlog. She came home, did her homework—including a bunch of past-due work—and then started cleaning her room, saying she couldn't believe we'd let her let it get that bad. We had to send her to our basement office at 1 a.m. because she was making so much noise vlogging while editing video.

Thank goodness she had a therapy session scheduled the next day. She's too old for me to go into her sessions, but I dropped her off, made eye contact with her therapist, and said, "She's super happy today?" with a shrug. Her therapist smiled and invited T in.

That evening, T mentioned in passing that she'd given her therapist permission to call us. Her therapist asked that we please take notes for her on what T was like that week, but that we do so without judgment as long as T was safe. I remember thinking, "As long as she's safe? Why wouldn't she be safe? She's finally coming out of this."

Well, within a few days, I understood. T was firing on all cylinders. She would walk in after school and decide she was hungry and start baking cookies. But then she'd be texting with a friend and decide to take the dog for a walk while she was texting, forgetting about the cookies in the oven. T thought it was funny when she walked in to my neighbor on the phone with me after the neighbor heard our smoke detectors go off, smelled the burning cookies from her yard, and let herself in with her key when no one answered her knocks. It was like T had no sense of remorse or understanding of what could have happened.

Right around that time, I found out from a mom back in Florida that, according to her daughter, T had been acting "crazy" the spring before we moved. Looking back, that was probably T's first hypomanic episode. We thought her erratic behavior, lack of sleep, and acting out were a reaction to the news that we were moving and to our house being on the market. But her friend's mom later told me that she'd found out after we'd moved that the argument T had had with that friend group was about some risky behavior on T's part and that the rest of them had been trying to tell her to knock it off. T had become enraged and said some pretty horrible things about them on social media. I really wish I'd known what was happening at the time because T is not a mean person, so that might have tipped me off that something more than the move had been bothering her.

When T's therapist eventually diagnosed her with bipolar II, T didn't believe her and initially rejected the diagnosis and any proposed treatment. But we were relieved. The diagnosis gave us context for what was going on and helped us help her.

T has accepted it now, especially once she connected it to hurting her former friends' feelings, and she has started sharing things about it on social media. She reached out and apologized to the former friends and told them about her diagnosis. She's mostly received support and validation there, so that's been good for her.

You may have noticed that many of these conditions have significant overlap both with one another and with typical teen behaviors. This is why it is important to trust your instincts if something feels off, listen if someone else brings up a concern, and seek a professional opinion if you are unsure of what is going on. The one consistent theme I've heard among those who were not diagnosed as having a clinical problem until they were older is some variation of "I wish I'd known and gotten treatment earlier; it helps to have the right support."

The American Psychiatric Association recommends checking in with a mental health professional if you see several of the following symptoms developing in your adolescent:

• **Sleep or appetite changes:** Dramatic sleep and appetite changes or decline in personal care.

• **Mood changes:** Rapid or dramatic shifts in emotions or depressed feelings, greater irritability.

• **Withdrawal:** Recent social withdrawal and loss of interest in activities previously enjoyed.

• **Drop in functioning:** An unusual drop in functioning, at school, work or social activities, such as quitting sports, failing in school or difficulty performing familiar tasks.

• **Problems thinking:** Problems with concentration, memory or logical thought and speech that are hard to explain.

• **Increased sensitivity:** Heightened sensitivity to sights, sounds, smells or touch; avoidance of over-stimulating situations.

• **Apathy:** Loss of initiative or desire to participate in any activity.

• **Feeling disconnected:** A vague feeling of being disconnected from oneself or one's surroundings; a sense of unreality.

• **Illogical thinking:** Unusual or exaggerated beliefs about personal powers to understand meanings or influence events; illogical or "magical" thinking typical of childhood in an [an older person].

• **Nervousness:** Fear or suspiciousness of others or a strong nervous feeling.

• **Unusual behavior:** Odd, uncharacteristic, peculiar behavior.

• **Changes in school or work:** Increased absenteeism, worsening performance, difficulties in relationships with peers and co-workers.

Whether you feel your Creative is dealing with elevated "typical" teen or tween issues or you have concerns that there may be a more serious mental health issue at play, therapy is a very beneficial tool that can instill your teen or tween Creative with skills they will use for life. For Creatives, therapy can assist in productivity. It can also reduce stress and assist with developing so many of the skills we have already covered, such as resilience, and it can help them assess and address anxiety and self-esteem regarding their art. It may also move the needle on time-management, setting goals, and reconnecting to the joy of their art. It can even help with improving their artistic output and overall performance.

In addition to Creative-specific benefits, therapy can help your teen or tween develop lifelong coping skills and can improve chronic stress related to and unrelated to their art. It can help with communication, interpersonal skills, and self-defeating behaviors, help improve moods and regulate emotions, and increase a teen or tween's ability to function in multiple areas of life.

Seeking help can seem daunting at times, but there are many ways to start seeking a good referral:

• Ask your teen or tween's primary care physician,

• Ask your Creative's school social worker or counselor,

• Ask a trusted friend,

• Ask other parents of teens or tweens,

• Call your insurance provider to ask for their in-network providers,

• Ask a trusted instructor (especially if you are seeking a therapist who understands the unique needs and pressure of Creatives or the creative process),

• Search reliable online databases such as Psychology Today or Mental Health Match, or

• Reach out to organizations that support your specific concerns.

An important note to consider: therapy is very personal—it is relationship-based. Talk to your Creative about the fact that, although therapy may feel uncomfortable at times (especially once the relationship is established and their therapist begins exploring more personal or difficult issues), if they don't feel a connection to the first person they meet with, it's perfectly acceptable for them to try a new therapist. They may need to meet with several a few times each before they find the right match, the therapist who they feel "gets" them and is able to help them address their concerns. When your Creative connects with the right therapist, they will discover that therapy is a lasting resource at their disposal for whenever life puts a bump in the road.

Chapter 9

Other Considerations

K was bullied and did not fit in during grade school. He suffered from anxiety and depression. His dog and his guitar were the only things that brought him joy. When he joined a contemporary music program, he found his people. He had a great teacher and found friends who were like him. Talented, kind, intense about the music, and smart. He flourished there. His friends are his community and his family and his people.

As a therapist and consultant working with parents and instructors of creative teens and tweens, I have seen several themes come up repeatedly. I think it's important to acknowledge these considerations and how they impact Creatives.

BULLYING

According to the National Center for Education Statistics, one out of every five—20 percent—students report being bullied. Boys are more often the victim of physical bullying, while girls report more incidents of being the victims of rumors or being intentionally excluded by a peer group. [1]

Recent studies report the following:

• Forty-one percent of students who have been bullied report that they feel the bullying will occur again.

• Of students who report being bullied:

  ○ Thirteen percent report being made fun of, called names, or insulted,

  ○ Thirteen percent were the victims of rumors,

  ○ Five percent were pushed, shoved, tripped, or spit on, and

  ○ Five percent were excluded from activities on purpose.

• More girls (24 percent) than boys (17 percent) report being bullied at school.

• One in five tweens (20 percent) report having been cyber-bullied, having cyberbullied someone else, or having witnessed cyberbullying.

• Of tweens who report being bullied, 50 percent report being bullied at school and 15 percent indicated they had experienced bullying online.

• Some teens and tweens will self-blame for the bullying.

Those who do are more likely to experience depression, prolonged victimization, and maladjustment.

Teens and tweens who are bullied are at greater risk for depression, anxiety, sleep problems, and lower academic achievement and are more likely to drop out of school.[2] They are twice as likely as their non-bullied peers to experience increased health issues including headaches and stomachaches.[3] Nearly 70 percent of tweens who have been cyberbullied reported that the abuse negatively impacted their physical health, their friendships, their schoolwork, and their view of themselves.[4]

Sherri Gordon, a bullying prevention expert, indicated that the types of kids who are most likely to be bullied include those who are successful, determined, intelligent, or creative.[5] As one of my clients said, "That's practically a universal description for so many teens and tweens in the arts."

This list of characteristics is significant in the context of encouraging creative kids to share their interests in a more public setting. There is a very real risk in sharing one's creative output, especially if your Creative is living in an area where artistic pursuits are not highly valued. As mentioned in chapter 7, asking our Creatives to perform, share, and exhibit something that may be very important to them is asking them to step into vulnerability—at an age where some peers may take advantage of this and bully them for this effort. Helping your teen or tween find peer support and a place to feel safe and protected, either in person or online, can be one of the most valuable tools you ever give them.

I almost pulled T out of school. He hadn't really fit in with the other boys in elementary school, but he had had his core few friends who stuck with him, and he enjoyed playing with them. Then middle school hit, and it was horrible. *Horrible.*

The middle school breaks the kids into smaller groups, and not one of his friends was in his, so he didn't see them other than at lunchtime. I want to cry every time I think about it. He was bullied the first week. He could never really say why—I think bullies can sense he won't fight back. They'd trip him and try to make him fall down in the hall. Then they'd try to shame him and call him clumsy. It was just so hard because he's this super-sensitive theater-loving kid and he just kept saying, "I don't know why they hate me."

Thank goodness the after-school theater program saved him. He found real friends there, and I noticed he wasn't having as many stomach issues before school once he started hanging out with those kids more. There's still a group of "popular" boys who are mean to him, but the physical bullying has decreased and he feels like he belongs somewhere.

Once, when he was walking home, two of the popular boys started following him and making fun of him. Thank goodness he happened to be passing one of the theater kids' houses, and a few of the kids were there on the porch and saw the bullying. These sweet kids called my boy over and invited him to hang out. When he said he couldn't, that he had to get home before his younger sister, they hopped off the porch and walked home with him. It was the first time he felt like he had real friends again. And those same kids really are his friends now—they invite him over.

It's a stretch financially, but we got an after-school sitter for my daughter so T can hang out with [his new friends] after school even when there aren't any theater rehearsals.

FITTING IN WITH THEIR PEER GROUP

The need to fit in, to be well-regarded by their peer group, makes teens and tweens especially vulnerable to peer pressure. They may be tempted to do anything, even things that are detrimental or self-destructive, to elevate or preserve their standing with their peers.

As parents, we are unfortunately limited in our influence against these struggles, which can be frustrating to watch. Though beginning to prioritize fitting in is a natural part of social skill development, it is important to keep an eye on the choices being made and watch for any signs of bullying. Beyond that, striving to keep the lines of communication open regarding how your Creative's artistic pursuits are being received by their peers can help with positive decision-making. It can also open the doors for you to have better insight if your teen or tween does not want to share their creative pursuits in an open forum. Understanding any negative feedback your Creative is receiving from their peers can allow you to encourage balanced decision-making skills.

The vast majority of teens and tweens will go through some periods of feeling as though they don't fully fit in. For you as their parent, this can become a concern if your Creative constantly feels there is no place they fit in. That can be another way of saying, "I don't feel emotionally safe." Tuning in to this, validating it, and empathizing with your teen or tween will help make your home a place where they can experience emotional security.

Ask your Creative to join you in looking for places where they are more likely to find some more connection with peers. Often, those may be places connected to their art. If they aren't finding connection in their current artistic community, consider branching out, trying the programs in a different town or online.

My husband's job requires us to move every two years or so. Mostly we love it, and the kids have learned so much. A played sports for a while, but over time he started drifting toward other things. He discovered he loved dance when we were living downtown in a major city, just blocks from a well-known studio. I took him there as a way to get his energy out in the winter and found that not only did he enjoy it, but he seemed to be really good at it.

From ages six to eleven, A danced wherever we went, but then we relocated to an area where, well, boys just don't dance. I thought this was ridiculous, and we were raising these worldly kids, so I figured I'd commit to driving the seventy minutes to the closest dance studio that offered a boys' class. That worked for about two months until all of the sudden, A said he wanted to quit. He just refused to discuss it; he was done.

After a month or so, I could tell he missed it, but he would just shake his head when I asked if he wanted to reconsider. Eight months later, we had a family meeting to discuss a potential move. We'd committed to not moving more than once every twenty-four months, but an amazing opportunity had come up outside Los Angeles, which is near where we'd hoped to land permanently—and this job had the potential to lead to that. My daughter wasn't thrilled but said that if we would promise to stay in that location for at least three years, she would be okay with it. But A's response surprised us. He had friends—he was always running out the door with a pack of boys in our subdivision. We'd given in and gotten him a cell phone mainly because we were tired of random numbers texting our phones to ask if he could go out. We thought he'd be really upset. But... when we said LA, he jumped up and said, "Yes!" When pressed, he only shrugged his shoulders.

Fast-forward to after the move. We're in an Airbnb while

our belongings are being moved and A comes bounding down the stairs and asks if I have plans that afternoon. Turns out he'd been researching dance opportunities and had found a drop-in class twenty minutes away. Not only that, but the reason he wanted to go there was to get his technique back and then he wanted to try out for the hip-hop team at the studio closer to our new home.

I agreed to take him if he would explain himself. He said that the boys in our last town had noticed a picture of him onstage in our family room and had laughed. He said that they weren't mean, but he could tell that that was because the picture was a few years old and they had thought it was something we had "made" him do when he was little. He told me he'd gone to class for another few weeks after that, but then he'd seen the younger sister of one of the boys at the studio and realized he'd heard the boys making fun of all the boys at their school who did anything other than sports. He had wanted to fit in, and that was more important to him than dance. That's why he was so happy we were back in a large city—many of his dance heroes were from LA, and he knew he could find people who accepted him as a dancer.

I had had no idea. Now that he was twelve, I wasn't really involved in his friendships the way I had been when he was younger, so I felt really bad that I hadn't pushed harder to understand what had happened, but I was so glad he was going back.

The desire to fit in is a normal developmental experience. As younger kids begin to enter their tween years, the limited interventions parents engage in in an effort to protect kids within their peer groups lessen. By middle school, tweens may be participating in extended networks, often engaging with peers their parents do not know. They begin to form new social communities, and this comes with the reality that not all relationships, friendships, or groupings are going to be equal. There will naturally be the tweens (and, later, teens) who are more sought after within the groupings—the more popular kids. Teens tend to be extra aware of how they are perceived by their peers and often link their happiness to this externally controlled scale.

BUILDING COMMUNITY

A theme that sometimes comes up with artistic kids is challenges in finding true friendships, peer connections, and/or a sense of community. For some, depending on their creative endeavor of choice, there may be a limited number of kids who are engaging in the same activity. Others may find they have a deeper interest in their creative art than their peers have. Some Creatives may see the world differently than their peers do or may want to spend their free time in creative activities that may not fit the mold of what their peers find enjoyable.

> S was really lonely for a long time. We lived in an area where sports and everything connected to sports was the main social outlet, and S just really had no interest in sports. Even though their peers seemed interested in seeing the anime characters they would draw, they were also labeled as "weird" for their interest in cosplay. We tried to limit their internet time, but we found an online class on anime and signed S up for it. It was a game changer. The kids all really enjoyed each other, and a few of them were in an online community group together. S begged and begged to be allowed to join.
>
> We agreed with some rules, including that they could only go on in the dining room, where we could monitor the interactions. Eventually, we allowed them to use the laptop

in their room with the door open because we could hear what was going on—all stuff that S had felt isolated about—sharing art, talking about cosplay makeup, discussing new episodes of shows they liked. I worried about so much time online, but it was, well, honestly more social than S had been.

We moved recently to a fairly large suburb, and now S has a few close in-person friends. They correct me when I say "real" friends because S is very clear that the online crew are real friends, and they are still really active in that community. I'm grateful [access to online communities] opened up more places S could hang out with people who understood what they loved.

Though there were some online options in the past, the offerings have exploded since 2020. With the normalization of learning remotely, there are many great answers to both expanding opportunities for skill development and connecting with like-minded peers. Opportunities to take classes, watch seminars, and participate in workshops have greatly increased. This is amazing and certainly can build an online community. But what if your Creative is craving in-person relationships?

Several parents I've spoken with were from areas without many options for their Creatives, or their Creatives had exhausted and outgrown the offerings that were available. Those parents and I explored many choices, including enrolling their children in weekend classes in neighboring towns or asking if their children might participate in classes with slightly older peers to keep them interested and make sure they were consistently interacting with others. One mom reported that she would have never thought she'd drive ninety minutes one way for a musical theater program, but she ended up agreeing to let her son try for eight weeks, the length of one show cycle. Part of the deal was that he had to get himself up and ready and have all his chores done before they hit the road at 8:20 a.m.

Honestly, as much as he loves musical theater, I didn't think W would make it very long, especially as winter was starting. But he kept his end of the bargain. I never had to remind him to do his chores, and I'd often find him doing them Friday evening so he could sleep in a little bit more. He was up, dressed, packed, and ready to go every day.

He lived for those Saturdays. From 10 a.m. to 3 p.m., he was happy and he had real friends. It was so good for him. I don't know why I had been so resistant. There were no real opportunities for young teens to be in shows near us. I had to remind myself that many of the people in our community were driving just as far or farther to attend their kids' football games.

I actually came to appreciate the time with my son, and once I realized I just couldn't take it away from him after the eight weeks, I found an online side hustle that I could do from the lounge area of the studio. It was a win-win. I would never have been able to totally focus [on a side hustle] without jumping up to do laundry or something for those hours at home, but I was making more than enough to cover the [travel] costs. My husband was usually gone with our younger son to whatever travel games he had. For the first time in quite a while, W felt like he was with his people and like he was making real progress, and he was so much happier.

FINDING THE RIGHT FIT

If your Creative pursues their art on more than a hobbyist level, meaning moving from no classes or very casual classes to more rigorous training with industry experts, teachers, or instructors, higher-level classes, and possibly mentors, chances are that, at some point, there will be a poor match. Every Creative will have different learning styles, different needs, different challenges, different approaches, and different levels of commitment. What do you do when your child comes to you and says, "I don't like this instructor?"

The reasons behind this may be varied. Though it may be tempting to take your Creative's "side," it's important to take a step back and ask *why* your Creative is unhappy. Some reasons I have seen that have come up:

• Classes were outside the Creative's comfort zone, bringing up new skills that were needed but challenging.

• A teacher was pushing to break bad habits formed when the Creative was much younger.

• An instructor was not "warm and fuzzy," even though the material was excellent and appropriate.

• Classes were at a bad time of day. (This has come up for both young children being moved up into more advanced classes later in the evening and older teens taking early weekend classes when they desperately need to catch up on sleep.)

• An instructor could not formally require but very clearly expected participation in additional classes and did not take the students who weren't enrolled in those classes as seriously as the others.

• Material moved too fast for the Creative's learning style.

• Classes were above or below the expected skill level.

• An instructor was verbally aggressive in communication, but only when other adults were not able to hear.

• An instructor gave bad advice and contradicted much of what was learned in previous training.

• The Creative and teacher had a difference in personality. (In this case, a super bubbly, upbeat, talkative Creative had a much more reserved and solemn teacher.)

• A teacher was extremely rigid in their approach and often expected things well above the students' skill level.

• An instructor did not like teaching anything other than advanced classes and told the intermediate class that teaching them was a waste of the instructor's time.

• An instructor would not allow students who did not achieve benchmarks to move forward.

• An instructor implied that if a student went against their family values to complete an assignment, the student would do better in a judged competition.

Some of these were legitimate reasons for wanting to reconsider the situation and consider making changes; others were growth opportunities that offered Creatives the chance to develop a growth mindset, take chances, and, yes, learn how to navigate failure and resilience.

There are several things you, as a parent, should consider —or advise your teen or tween to consider—when starting with a new instructor, studio, class, etc. In fact, you may wish to keep these things in mind even if your Creative doesn't have an urgent need to make a switch. It's easy to get comfortable with one instructor or studio and become complacent about doing due diligence about who will be working with your Creative, and sometimes it's worth considering whether even a beloved instructor is still the best match for your Creative as they become older or develop increased skills.

Get recommendations from people you trust if at all possible. If you don't know anyone connected to the art of choice, do your research. Look online and become a detective. See if you can find any information to help inform your decision. If your Creative is looking to move into more serious training, check if you can find information regarding the instructor's training, education, work experience, endorsement, special certifications, awards, or anything else that suggests they are prepared to teach at a higher level.

These should not be the only criteria for finding an appropriate instructor or studio. Depending on your Creative's needs, sometimes instructors with little formal training may be able to forge a connection with them that creates an amazing learning environment. Experience, great interpersonal skills, self-education, and enthusiasm for teaching may be the only qualifications that some of the best instructors who come into your Creative's life need depending on what skills your Creative is seeking to enhance.

Of course, you and your Creative can do all the due diligence you can, and it still will not guarantee a great match or experience. Pay attention to any changes in your Creative's attitude or mood as they start with a new instructor. Ask questions, even if they are met with resistance. If something isn't right, your Creative will know you are available to talk and process what is happening, and you can help them determine if their current environment is the right place for them to keep developing their skills.

As your Creative becomes more skilled and serious about their art, be wary of false promises. If someone is promising they can give your Creative amazingly fast progress, fame, fortune, or guaranteed entrance into any school… politely walk away. Trust your gut. If you or your Creative is uncomfortable and can't get past that feeling, then move on. You do not need a "reason" to leave if something feels truly off. No one can do their best work if they don't feel safe—nor should they be asked to stay in an environment that makes them feel that way. They should feel validated and supported in whatever setting they are in, and they should have clarity around the feedback they receive.

> D would make a choice in what to play and how to play it, and he knew why he was playing it that way, but he felt that it wasn't understood or appreciated in a certain setting. He didn't feel the feedback made sense; he felt it didn't address the fact that he made certain choices on purpose. And I could see it sometimes messed with his confidence.
>
> Now, I think, after doing some other things—like a composition workshop and various jazz ensembles—that he feels like he's met people who acknowledge that he plays a certain way out of choice. And now he feels confident in choosing instructors who support his way of approaching things and push him in ways that make sense to him.
>
> I'm glad we made him try new things. And I'm glad we didn't make him stay when it just didn't feel right.

Chapter 10

Emotional and Physical Safety on Social Media

We had told our kids that they couldn't have social media accounts until high school. L was pretty upset about that and asked if she could start a YouTube channel and TikTok account if we approved all of her posts. My husband is a teacher and he said no way. He said it was too addictive, that kids were losing studying and sleeping time on it. L was frustrated and said that all she wanted to do was post singing covers.

L tried to sneak a TikTok account, and when my husband found out, he took away her phone and replaced it with a flip phone. L was furious because she used her phone to record videos. I finally gave her my old disconnected phone for videos. She was incredibly angry with us for quite a while, but she finally seemed to get over it.

Then, this past summer, she entered a local singing contest with some great prizes, opportunities to sing in public, a chance to work with some producers—all things she was desperate to do. Well, she came in second place, even though it was clearly very, very close. Later, she found out from someone close to the contest that they likely chose the other girl over her because of the other girl's social media presence and following. The girl had been putting out lots of TikTok videos, and she had amassed a good-size following. She'd also been posting about the contest during the entire process. My daughter was so angry with us, she was screaming and yelling and saying we didn't get it, we didn't have a clue how things worked in the industry nowadays and that our old-fashioned view of the world was costing her opportunities.

I'm not sure what to think. I started researching, and it does seem like there is some validity to what she's saying. I'm seeing singers who are getting known because of TikTok, and now I feel bad, like we held her back and she has to play catch-up. I'm not sure what to do.

YouTube is the most popular entertainment platform among teens ages thirteen to seventeen.[1] While tween social media usage jumped during the pandemic, teens spend nearly five times as much time on social media as tweens. A recent study of thirteen- to twenty-four-year-olds found that 66 percent of participants felt comfortable on social media platforms, and over half admitted to spending too much time on social media. Up to 66 percent of the respondents in other studies reported that social media had a direct impact on depression and self-esteem.[2]

By now, it is common knowledge that social media algorithms are designed to keep the user engaged. By predicting what content will be of interest to the user and suggesting that content, social media platforms easily achieve their goal of keeping the user glued to the screen, consuming more and more, thus generating income for the platform.[3]

For any parent of a teen or tween, the question of when and how to allow social media access is a complicated one.

For parents of Creatives in particular, many of whom will see that their artistic idols have a social media presence, there is the added question of whether you allow or even encourage your teen or tween to post or interact online related to their art.

IS SOCIAL MEDIA THE RIGHT CHOICE FOR YOUR CREATIVE?

Social media can serve as social proof. It can be a means to develop a fan base without leaving your home. The barriers to recognition in so many creative arts have been lowered by the ability to post content demonstrating one's skills. The ability to access lessons, information, and tutorials—often for free or at a reasonable cost—is vast and seemingly never-ending. By limiting your Creative's access, are you putting them at a disadvantage when compared to their peers of the same age?

There is no good answer here. There are those (often in older generations) who will swear up and down that social media is not necessary, that emphasis on behind-the-scenes training and skill development, pursuing consistent opportunities in emotionally safe environments, and developing healthy, consistent work habits is the best, most expedient route to growth and that social media shouldn't be used until a Creative is older. No one can deny all of these things are essential for developing excellence.

Yet the younger—and very vocal—generation has made an argument that, with social media being the language of youth, those who fail to have some presence online are missing a large opportunity. There appears to be increasing validation for this argument in certain circumstances. Following up on L's story above, L's mother came to me because the relationship between L and her parents around her singing had become very stressful. L's mother had been pretty upset with the people who had put on the contest, saying nowhere had it been mentioned that social media following would factor into the winner choice. It was only when I pointed out that a winner with some sort of social media following would be instant marketing for the contest, and that choosing a winner with a following may have helped the organizers feel confident that the work they were going to do with the winning artist would be getting out to a larger audience, that the mother finally understood why the judges may have been influenced by the knowledge that the winner had more of a social media following than L did. Whether allowing social media to impact the winner choice was right or wrong, the winner's following only served the contest in a positive way.

This does not mean a parent should allow their Creative to jump into social media connected to their art of choice without serious consideration. There are just as many down-sides to social media as there are upsides. As a clinician, consultant, and parent, I have struggled with this debate. The answers are varied and highly individual. A few examples of questions I ask parents who are considering whether to allow social media for their Creatives include:

• What is your teen/tween's maturity level?

• What type of content are you comfortable with your teen/tween consuming? Posting?

• What apps does your teen/tween want access to and why?

• What does your teen/tween see as the purpose of having access to social media?

• Will your teen/tween have an account for their art and a separate private one for their in-real-life friends and peers?

• What are the ground rules, and will these change over time?

• Do you want to preapprove posts on a public account?

• Will you have access to the account? How will your teen/tween feel about that choice? If you will not have access, how will you monitor the account?

• Do you feel your teen/tween would be able to manage and set boundaries around the emotional downsides of posting—trolls, negativity, potential emotional abuse?

• Do you feel that, if those things came up, your teen/tween would come to you to let you know?

• Does your teen/tween truly have a good grasp of the downsides of social media?

• What is your teen/tween hoping to gain with a social media presence connected to their art?

• Do you feel you have a good working knowledge of the social media platforms your teen/tween wants to access?

Conversations about social media safety—both emotional and physical—are absolutely necessary, in particular for younger tweens, but also with teens. If you as a parent have limits and boundaries, these need to be clearly stated up front, and you need to make it clear that you reserve the right to tighten or loosen these boundaries as needed. You must carefully think about (and continually reassess) how to manage trolls, when your teen or tween needs to take breaks, whether to set your teen or tween's profile to public or private, and other considerations regarding appropriate social media usage.

WHAT TO CONSIDER BEFORE GETTING ONLINE

We live in an undeniable social media age. Young people born after 2005 were born into the world of social media; they have never known life without it. Just as television changed the way people interacted with the news and entertainment, the advent and dominance of social media in modern culture has led to a major shift in the way teens and tweens consume their news and entertainment. Studies show that more than half of teenagers get their news and current events from watching videos on social media rather than directly from news organizations.[4]

Regardless of what you and your Creative decide is an appropriate approach to social media in your family, in addition to doing traditional due diligence where general internet safety is concerned, here are just a few things to consider regarding your Creative and their social media presence.

The first is that you, as the parent, need to understand the basics of how whichever social media they are using for their art works. I've worked with parents who had a cursory working knowledge but had never really explored the platform their Creatives were actively engaged with. Set up your own account. Poke around and find out how things work and what the various features are, and learn the lingo for the platform. Understand how people communicate with one another, how to block unwanted users, and how to report inappropriate interactions.

Navigating Online Communication

Talk to your Creative in advance about how to respond to DMs regarding their art. Have a plan of action in place for how to respond, one that includes both how to vet these communications and how to respond and who will handle this. Remind your Creative to never give out any personal contact information, no matter what is being said or what opportunity is allegedly being offered in a message. Discuss how people and organizations representing legitimate opportunities will never pressure them to give out their phone number or address, and make sure they know that legitimate entities will be very comfortable with a parent contacting them (or, in the case of most reputable companies, will even insist on doing business in this way if your Creative is under eighteen).

Here are some examples of spam DMs underage Creatives have received (shared with me by their parents):

> Hi dear artist. I'm a professional digital marketer and music promoter. Want to promote spotify for large audience?

> Hi! Wonderful work! We are seeking unknown 2D-artists to create characters for a game. The characters you develop will live on as part of the game forever! Respond with a character drawing and we will let you know if it is the type of work we need and of it is we will tell you how to send the information we need to set up your payment

> Wow! Amazing skills - you have what it takes to become famous. we are looking for super good triple-threat new actors like you - we can teach you the secrets of standing out and getting casted in the next big Disney feature open casting call. Interested? Link in bio

> Hey listened to your music you are fire! If you have any new material we are running a talent search contest—all expenses paid recording album at our studio—travel and lodging included.

> I just wanted to make you aware that your YT audience is low. Your content is awesome. If you want I can promote your audience. Real and organic targeted.

> Hello! I came across your account and I love how you rep for BAND MUSIC. We represent arts and clients who also rep BAND MUSIC and are looking for influencer ambassadors.

> Hello Beautiful Girl! We saw your page and beautiful dancer body and think you would be perfect to model for us. Click on the link in our bio and fill out the form for new models and we'll send you some merch to try on and see if you like it

Some questions for you and your Creative to ask when your Creative receives DMs from unfamiliar accounts include the following:

• Is the DM poorly written?

• Do they have thousands of followers but almost no likes on posts? This can be a sign of fake followers. Or do they have no followers, or very few?

• If they do have followers, who are those followers? Do they seem to be people who would legitimately be following that type of account?

• Do they follow your account? How long have they been a follower? Have they actively and appropriately commented on your public posts in the past?

• Does what they are offering feel too good to be true (especially for someone who is unknown or does not have a huge following)?

• Are they overusing industry buzzwords to get your attention?

• Are their posts related or relevant to the industry they claim to be in?

• Are they asking for immediate and/or untraceable payment?

While some legitimate inquiries may raise a red flag here and there, if you notice an account or message has several traits that you find suspicious, then it would be wise to proceed with caution. Remember, these DMs are allegedly from a person or company that has something to offer you. Generally, companies who are actually in a position to promote your Creative are going to have a dedicated social media manager who will send an appropriate message that they would be happy for an adult to read.

Even more sinister, but a real concern, are adults who are interested in developing a personal relationship with minors. This is a DM received by a young male child actor.

> Hello handsome boy! Your music is so good
> – Can we be friends? I'm don't have a lot of
> people to talk to can I send you a message?
> Do you have C $ s h @ p p? I want to send
> you a gift.

That Creative's mother runs his account and was quickly able to determine that the message was from a middle-aged adult male who only follows young or teenage boys. When the mother asked why he had a feed full of often shirtless prepubescent boys, the man claimed he was looking for "young male models." Yes, this happens. You must 100 percent be prepared to watch for predatory adults, including adults pretending to be teens or tweens. You must be hyper-vigilant and teach your teen or tween to be so as well.

Some of the questions you should ask yourself when vetting unknown profiles are:

• Does the person who sent the DM have something other than a photo of themselves as their profile image?

• If not, are there other photos on the account of the alleged owner?

• If not, what are the images of? Young people? Odd jokes? Anything that feels off?

• Do they ask for your Creative's age? This is only appropriate if it's something along the lines of "Hey, if you are under 18, we'd need to speak to a parent before we could move forward" in the case of someone offering a service or opportunity.

• Are they offering an excessively complimentary comment

in the DMs while keeping a more appropriate tone on the main page?

• Do they only have one "type" they follow? For example, are the majority of the accounts they follow young teens or tweens with a specific look or style of dress?

• Are they claiming to have all of the exact same interests as your Creative? "Hi! I see you have a cat and you like video games. I have a cat and like video games—we are so alike!"

• Do they inquire about your Creative's family life? This can be a ploy to determine whether your Creative has adults in their life who are involved, aware, and protective.

• Are they requesting photos? They can see your Creative's profile photos. No one should ever ask for additional photos/selfies. Be especially in tune with any requests that they pose in their bedroom, especially on their bed, or take bathroom selfies.

• Are they making inappropriate requests, such as requests for your Creative's phone number, email address, physical address, or other ways to connect, such as other social media platforms where a parent may not have access?

As a parent, it is important for you to vet the profiles and accounts of anyone who is reaching out to your Creative—especially on a public account. Trust your gut and, if it doesn't feel right, err on the side of caution. Deleting, blocking, and reporting anyone who makes you uncomfortable in any way will help to keep your Creative safe.

Influencer Marketing: What Your Creative Needs to Know

Another conversation I would strongly encourage you to have with your Creatives is about what it means to be an "influencer." When brands reach out to an unknown artist, chances are, at the very least, they are offering a bad deal, but worse, they may be engaging them in a relationship with negative returns. Though micro-influencers (people on social media with between one and four thousand followers) are becoming increasingly popular with brands, it's still important to remember that true influencers are known for their reputation, knowledge, and expertise on a topic or for having large organic followings. Unless your Creative fits one of these descriptions, I would urge you both to look carefully at any unsolicited offers. You should also familiarize yourself with the legal implications and requirements of any brand contracts.

Remind your Creative that high-quality studios, galleries, marketers, and businesses will not be doing a keyword search to find unknown teen and tween artists, especially not anyone with under fifty to one hundred thousand organic followers. Also remind them that followers can be bought, so even if an inquiry comes from an account with one hundred thousand "followers," that does not mean that the account is legitimate or credible. Learn how to vet accounts—everyone starts somewhere, some small, so a legit start-up *could* be behind the request, but you need to learn how to figure that out.

Brand ambassadors are another social media phenomenon that has grown exponentially over the past few years. Brand ambassadors are individuals whom a company feels represents their attitude, voice, face, and tone. It is possible that your teen or tween might be approached to be a brand ambassador, especially if they post often about using and loving a certain product and tag the company in their posts on a regular basis.

Again, this is a situation where you as the adult must do your due diligence and make sure that the offer is legitimate. If your Creative is expected to purchase their own product, pay for shipping, or sell any product in any way, I would encourage you to walk away. Be sure that you and your Creative understand what is being asked of them. They will likely be expected to commit to a certain number and type of posts in a specific time frame in exchange for "free" product. Make sure your Creative will be able to meet these requirements without experiencing additional stress or pressure.

You and your Creative should also be sure there is no conflict of interest—for example, if your Creative's dance team is sponsored by a dancewear company, will it create a problem if they promote another company's products? Or, if the agreement with the dancewear company requires your Creative to only post images where they are wearing the company's products, would this prevent them from posting about performing with their dance team? And what happens if their studio posts an image of them wearing the competing brand's team outfit? It's a lot to consider, and what may seem like an easy, fun way to get some "free" product may not be worth the effort. Before considering jumping into this world, you and your Creative should spend time learning about and understanding how to read and negotiate contracts, and you should both ensure that you understand terms such as "in perpetuity" (don't do it), "usage rights," and "exclusivity," just to name a few.

WHAT TO TALK ABOUT BEFORE YOUR TEEN GETS ONLINE

It's also important to be prepared for the potential drawbacks that come with posting to social media. For dancers in particular, I would consider it imperative that you have a conversation about the impact of potential negative comments regarding their appearance or body *before* your Creative begins posting. Trolls are very real and very cruel. If you or your Creative feel they would not be able to tolerate this type of vitriol, then you may want to reconsider engaging in any public social media connected to dance, or you may wish to be very vigilant about what type of clothing is being worn in your Creative's videos.

Visual artists may feel a great temptation to digitize their art and share it on platforms such as Instagram and TikTok. Artists can livestream as they create art, sharing their process and gaining a true following. Although this may seem like an amazing opportunity for them to get their artwork "out there," there are concerns about doing so that you should discuss with their Creative. Digital art theft is a real and increasing problem. If your visual artist is concerned with ownership of their art, you should familiarize yourself with image copyright on social media and make sure you understand the limits of what can be done if your Creative's rights are violated.

If your Creative is already a content creator, all of the above still applies. While you may both be well versed in many of the pitfalls of social media, it never hurts to revisit the concerns. Keep the lines of communication open. As a parent, have your own account and subscribe to outlets such as podcasts, blogs, newsletters, and YouTube channels that talk about the content creator world. It's an ever-changing landscape, so you should never become complacent about monitoring your Creative's content. *All of it.* Long-form, short-form, photos, tweets—you want to see it all. Keep an eye on the comments as well.

Whatever decision you make, whether you allow your Creative to create social media accounts, ask them to wait, or come to another compromise, stay in communication with your Creative about the variable world of social media. Keep in mind that the choices and limitations you may settle on with a ten-year-old will most likely need to be revisited just a few years later. Keep checking in and understanding what your Creative's current social media preferences are and how they are feeling. Remain open and receptive to their perspective to avoid your Creative choosing to sneak social media accounts without your knowledge. Reinforce the need for them to protect their own privacy and reputation. It is also important to remind them to be aware of how they treat others—if a comment is something they wouldn't say to the recipient's face, then it is not something they should say on social media.

And as their parent, let them know that, although you will be following their accounts, you promise not to violate their privacy and you will refrain from posting information about them without their permission. Let them know you will avoid making embarrassing comments—no matter how much of a place of love they may come from—on their accounts.

Part III

Supporting Your Creative's Growth

Chapter 11

Being the Parent Your Creative Needs

Most of us want to be the best parents we can be. Before our children are born, many of us read, study, and imagine what this parenting journey might look like. Yet, when our children arrive into our lives, so many of our plans go out the window. Even when they're tiny infants, it is clear that our children come to us as their own beings, with their own wants, needs, and desires.

I have been known to joke that when my kids were little I was an accidental co-sleeper. Sleep training was a common practice at that time, and as a well-read new mom, I had heard the warnings regarding "allowing" your infant to be reliant on parents to fall or stay asleep. I was ready to ensure that my infants would be great sleepers capable of self-soothing.

Then my first son was born eight weeks premature. After he was discharged from the NICU after three weeks of bottle feedings, nursing was a challenge. Once things were finally going well, the last thing I was going to do was disrupt the precious cycle we'd developed that allowed me to get one hour or so of sleep every three hours. When I would move my son to his crib, he would wake instantly and cry to be held. He'd grown used to being around people, even while sleeping, while in the hospital. It only took a few nights of constantly interrupted sleep for all involved before I saw that this was not in his best interest, nor mine.

So he'd slept right next to me—in a co-sleeper, where I could reach over and soothe him quickly. It was a swift learning curve. I valued sleep for both of us in the short term over sleep training for him. I knew almost immediately that I was a better, calmer, and, most importantly, happier mom if I was well-rested. And my son was thriving after being born at three pounds and three ounces, so I felt that trusting my instinct was working and there was no need to change things until he was a bit older. Eventually, I was able to move him to a crib in a way that felt right for both of us. I also learned some mothers experience the exact opposite journey—they intend to co-sleep but find neither they nor their children are well rested when their children are next to or in their beds, and thus, early sleep training becomes their path to being better, calmer, and happier moms and babies.

Ultimately, it comes down to looking at who we are and what we feel our children need and doing our best to adjust and make it work.

Meeting our kids where they are, figuring out what they need, and working to adjust accordingly is the constant job of parenting. Parenting a Creative has its own rewards and challenges that can require a special kind of support, flexibility, and patience.

Here are a few suggestions on how to strive to be the parent your individual Creative needs. Some of these concepts are based on the practice of Autonomy Supportive Parenting, while others are concepts I came to embrace through observing and working with Creatives and their families.

PROVIDE UNCONDITIONAL LOVE—AND AVOID THE CONDITIONAL LOVE TRAP

Some of you may be thinking, "Um, yeah, I provide unconditional love all the time." And I believe you. I also know from working with teens and tweens over the years that it may not always feel that way to your Creative. Unconditional love can be tricky.

Unconditional love is not telling your Creative they are "amazing, wonderful, outstanding!" all of the time. It is not telling them coming in tenth place in a competition they desperately wanted to do well in to get a scholarship is "no big deal." Because it *is* a big deal to them.

Unconditional love is creating an environment of trust and respect, where you can discuss the bumps in the road from a loving and supportive place. If you approach your child saying, "That was amazing!" after they completely tanked onstage, they won't believe your feedback. They will either assume you are trying to cheer them up (which can then cue them that their performance was *so bad* their parent had to lie about it to them) or they will think you really have no ability to assess a successful versus less-than-successful performance.

The parent who comes at the situation with unconditional love may focus on what was good about the effort—"You worked really hard, and we are really proud of you."—or validate their Creative's experience—"That must have been really challenging. You seem upset, and I get that, but we are really impressed with you sticking with it."

It can be easy to slip into a conditional love trap in moments when we are feeling frustrated. Chances are you've done it—I know I have (never intentionally, and I've had to take a beat to really hear how I was expressing my frustration or aggravation). This may sound like:

- "We pay all of this money for lessons, and you don't even bother to do the work they asked for?"

- "Your sister manages to get into the car with all of her dance stuff on time every day! Why can't you manage to do the same?"

- "Is that really what you're wearing for the performance?"

- "I'm sorry, but we are not purchasing you that new gear we promised unless you prepare better for the next competition."

Conditional love can easily lead your Creative into a shame spiral, generate a fixed mindset, or push the perfectionist into self-doubt—"I can't do anything right, so why even try?" Conditional love is hurtful and destructive, and if it is a frequent occurrence in your interactions, they will stop looking to you as a trusted source of support.

If you find yourself falling into this trap in an effort to get your Creative to make a behavior change, remind yourself that your Creative is likely to hold onto the behavior even more when they feel the request is coming from a place of conditional love. They are also more likely to avoid sharing what they are working on and turn away from rather than toward you when they are struggling. This is an especially concerning dynamic because it will likely translate into other areas in their life, possibly to the point where, if they are in trouble or need help, they may not feel safe approaching you.

Unconditional love sets you, the parent, up as your child's

biggest ally. It means you accept and support their personality quirks, even when deep down inside, you may be thinking, "Really, this is how we're doing this? *Okaaaaay...*" Unconditional love makes your home a safe and emotionally healthy environment in which your Creative can learn, make mistakes, and grow in their art.

Going back to the previous examples of what conditional love may sound like, reframing these same emotions from a place of unconditional love might sound like this:

- "I've noticed you haven't been doing what your teacher asked for. Is there a reason? Is there something happening that isn't working for you?"

- "Is there a way that we can make it easier for you to get out the door for dance on time? I know for me, it helps if I make a list of what I need the next day and get it ready the night before."

- "I love that you have your own style. I don't know what the expectations are for what you are all wearing to the performance, but I trust that you do and that you feel good with your choice."

- "I'm glad you want to keep going even when things didn't turn out great. Let's figure out when to get you the gear we promised you."

WORK TOWARD INDEPENDENT, AGE-APPROPRIATE EDUCATED DECISIONS

When your Creative was younger, encouraging them to make age-appropriate decisions was important, but the weight of any missteps with those decisions wasn't particularly significant. It begins to hit much harder when they move into the teen and tween years. Asking your six-year-old if they want to take the drawing class or the pot-throwing class is rooted in exploration and new experiences. Whichever they choose, in the vast majority of cases, there will be no detrimental impact on their overall goals. But as they grow into the tween years, the decisions they make begin to take on much more weight.

Encourage your tween to make educated decisions. Teach them to research and think critically about their choices. Discuss the benefits of one class over another. Has your tween consistently stuck to the areas in their art where they feel most comfortable and confident? Now is the time to talk to them about the benefits of developing skills in other supporting or concurrent abilities they may need if they want to progress. If they tend to avoid your advice, encourage them to discuss their choices with their instructors or other experts or mentors in their art.

As your tween moves into the teen years, they should be taking increasing responsibility for researching and advocating for the steps they take in their art. Allowing your teen the space they need to make decisions, even when you can see the negative implications that some of those decisions may have, can be incredibly scary. Suddenly, it may really matter if they choose to take the easier and more enjoyable Art Appreciation over the more rigorous but foundational AP Art History class, especially if they are leaning into the idea of an art career. But they will never learn how to make these decisions—and learn from their mistakes—if you do not back off and allow them to take responsibility for their own research and priorities.

Inevitably, there will come more and more moments where hard decisions about what makes sense within their art will arise. Does your Creative stay with the teacher or studio they have known and loved forever but may be outgrowing, or do they try to find what they need within that situation? Do they go to the intensive, exclusive camp they were admitted to that may elevate their skills in their art, or do they have one last summer with all of their friends at their traditional sleepaway camp? Do they stay for the final scholarship-offering competition of the season, or do they miss it to travel to a family wedding?

The majority of the parents I have spoken to report that their child's interest in their art was evident from a young age, even if they didn't engage in it consistently until they were older. For some, the child found their passion on their own and began asking for equipment, lessons, and activities related to that passion. For others, the parents may have introduced them to their art by signing their child up for extracurricular activities, but the casual interest flipped into a child-driven passion pursuit. All three of my boys leaned heavily into music and creative play when they were preschoolers. Because they were the ones driving their interests in the early stages, it was easy to allow them to make their own choices. There was limited potential loss if they made choices we didn't fully agree with. Yet, as they got older, the choices began to matter more.

When allowed to make their own decisions, your Creative has the space to own that decision and the outcome. Learning to trust themselves, or to trust that, even if a decision didn't turn out the way they'd hoped, they can learn and recover from that choice, is an invaluable life skill.

Z loved her ballet studio, and she did really well there—so well that they really pushed to move her into the pre-pro program versus the recreational one as soon as she was eligible. She was reluctant, and we basically told her that if that was where she would learn the most, we wanted her to move up. She excelled, but the higher she moved up, the less she seemed to be enjoying it.

Finally, one day, she came to us and said that the rigorous training was causing her to lose some of her love of dance. This time, she was older, so we felt like it was her decision to make. It was hard, I won't lie. We'd invested a lot of time, money, and sacrifice for her dance, but we took a deep breath and asked ourselves, "What is there to gain by forcing her to keep going?" So she quit.

She said she missed dancing after a few months, and, to our surprise, she asked if she could try a few lessons at a modern dance studio she'd heard about in the city. We agreed, and it was there that she found her love for dance again. I'm so glad we let her make her own choice and didn't push her to stay at her previous studio—we had thought about it, but landed on it needing to be her decision. I think the fact that we left it up to her made it so she didn't need to do the teenage pushback thing. Now she's back to wanting to major in dance. And honestly, what she's doing now is no less rigorous—she's back on a pre-pro track—but it fits who she is and what she wants so much better.

HELP YOUR CHILD FEEL COMPETENT

Another benefit of allowing your teen or tween to make age-appropriate decisions is that, by encouraging them to apply critical-thinking skills and decide what they feel is best for themselves in their relationship to their art, you are saying, "I trust you to do what you think is best for yourself, your art, your happiness, and your well-being."

In order to survive navigating the world, learning to feel (and actually become) competent when making decisions is essential. I do not know a single person who can't look back at their life and find example after example of choices they made that may not have worked out the way they'd hoped. But at the same time, over time, most people come to trust themselves to make decisions and manage and learn from the outcomes.

As a parent, you need to set guidelines for younger children, and sometimes, you must set hard limits. You may have to say, "This is the class you need right now, and though you may not enjoy it, we as your parents understand the benefit." As your children mature, you move to offering fewer hard limits and more guidelines and general suggestions, and eventually you step back and allow your children to largely make their own choices. If you gradually increase the type and scope of the decisions they make from early childhood through their tween years, they develop competence and confidence in their decision-making abilities. Ideally, as your Creative moves into their later teen years, you will have moved into trusting them to make decisions about their creative development—even when you are quietly questioning the rationale behind their choices.

Even if you are reading this and thinking, "We haven't done a lot of that. Up until now we've largely guided their decisions," it's never too late. Sit down with your Creative and let them know you have seen their skill development and growth and you feel they are ready to take more responsibility for choices in their art. Talk about doing due diligence and research, being able to explain to themselves the "why" of their choices (even if it's as simple as "It's a fun class that I always wanted to take"), and support them in those choices.

At times, this is scary—and challenging. I know with my own boys, as they get older, it only becomes more complicated. I know they need to make their own choices, living with and working through any positive and negative consequences. Yet it can be hard to take a back seat when I have a strong (and, in my mind, much more informed) opinion on how they should proceed.

But I also know I would be doing them no favors by constantly taking learning opportunities, challenges, obstacles, and failures out of the way for them. Not only would they not learn their own lessons and not learn resilience from missteps, but I would be undermining their sense of competence. The best gift I can give them is to allow them space to build their internal sense of competence. By letting them make certain choices, find their own solutions, and trust their instincts on what feels right to them, I'm not only equipping them to enjoy and excel in their art on their own terms, but I'm also teaching lessons that will benefit them throughout adulthood.

As your Creative gets older, your job is to learn to bite your tongue when they leave their end-of-the-semester major art project to the last minute, even when you know they will be stressed, frustrated, and likely not to receive the grade they are capable of because they believe this is their "easy" subject. If you harass them and force them to get it done, they will believe the outcome would have been the same had they been allowed to do it later and they could have managed just as well at the last minute. Thus, there would be no lesson learned about planning and time-management—until the next time, where the consequences of this type of mismanagement might be much larger.

Support, validate, and nurture new skills as they emerge. When you see your Creative working hard to master a skill, be sure to let them know that you noticed, that you are aware of how hard they worked, and that you can see or hear the progress. It may seem obvious, but we sometimes make the mistake of assuming that, just because our teens or tweens are old enough to know they made progress, they don't need or appreciate the same cheerleading we did for them when they were younger. This is simply not true. They may act as though they don't care, but time and time again, teens and tweens have told me when their parents notice and comment on their improvements, and they very much appreciated the validation.

When your Creative makes a mistake but works their way through it, praise them. It's important to continually reinforce the idea that mistakes are a necessary step toward improved skills. In elementary school, they may have been taught to reframe "FAIL" as "First Attempt In Learning." Again, just because they are getting older does not in any way mean they don't need reminders that missteps are part of learning and you are proud of them for continuing to work at a new skill, even when it's challenging.

When mistakes happen, ask or point out to your Creative how they made choices to manage or mitigate those mistakes in the future. For one of my sons, slowing down when learning a new piece of music was a big hurdle. He wanted to jump into a piece and have it sound just like it did on his streaming service. It took time and patience for him to realize just how slowly (and frequently) he should run a piece in sections before beginning to speed up. But once he really embraced this approach, he discovered it decreased the time it took him to learn new music and he made far fewer errors this way. We made sure to let him know we saw and appreciated how he had grown and learned from previous missteps.

When your Creative struggles to make choices or doubts their competence, give examples of the choices they have made in the past and how they managed and learned from the outcomes. There is not one skill they have mastered that they have not had to work at on some level. I find we all tend to forget this at times, especially when we are dealing with the frustration of working to learn or master a new skill that is not coming easily in spite of hard work and focus. A gentle

"I know this is really frustrating," followed up with an example of another struggle they managed to find a way to work through, can help them find the motivation to keep working at it.

Remind yourself that if we empower them to feel respected and competent, they will ultimately be motivated to develop and practice the skills they need to manage their own lives and challenges as young adults.

C was a largely self-taught graphic designer for many years. My husband and I are lawyers—we knew nothing about that world—but C loved it and researched on his own and found opportunities to learn.

From online workshops to summer camps, he advocated for his passion, and he even convinced a camp to let him in a year under the age cutoff based on his portfolio. To be clear, we never used the word "portfolio"—he'd figured out that that was the barrier to entry in many circles, and he'd put one together for himself. It was that type of independence and tenacity that helped us be pretty hands-off with his decisions. I mean, we vetted and monitored for safety, but usually, C was pretty good at finding online communities that supported him and suggested places for him to keep learning.

When I was starting my new business, my husband and I were talking about how much money I should plan to spend on my new website and branding. C looked at me and said, "Will you let me do it? It would be great for my portfolio." Secretly I was a little hesitant, but I knew that he was talented and that if he was really into something he generally excelled. We agreed that instead of spending the money on a professional web designer and branding company, we'd use the money for a course on WordPress for him.

He picked what he thought he would need, and honestly,

I was shocked with what he came back with. Three days later, he sent me various logos and color palettes to choose from. I picked my favorite, and he tweaked it to make it something I really loved. Then, a few days after that, he told me he had my "beta" website up. It was great. Exactly what I needed to get started. We told him over and over how impressed we were, what an amazing job he had done. I've happily recommended him to other friends, which has made him so happy.

You know those moments that make you cry? Well, he was talking to a friend who wasn't feeling supported at home, and I overheard him say, "Yeah, my mom and dad really trust me to do a good job. I'm really lucky they totally support me figuring things out."

WORK ON EMPATHY AND ACTIVE LISTENING SKILLS

So many parents have said to me, "I have empathy for them on this, *but...*"

This really demonstrates the fact that many people may feel they understand what empathy is, but they may be getting it wrong in practice even if the underlying intention is right. Empathy is the ability to understand or consider another person's point of view, thoughts, and feelings in a situation without judgment, rather than just focusing on our own.

I often find myself explaining the difference between sympathy—which is rooted in pity or sorrow and maintains a degree of emotional distance ("Oh wow, you must be so embarrassed!")—versus empathy. Empathy is rooted in not only understanding but also sharing another person's emotional experience ("Ouch. I've had something similar happen, and it was so hard. I'm so sorry. It sucks.").

When a parent says, "I have empathy for them on this, *but…*" I usually follow up by reviewing empathy versus sympathy. The "but" immediately shifts the statement from a place of emotional connection to one of observing what is happening from a more distanced stance, and it implies judgment. When that happens, your Creative senses your distance from what they are feeling.

Dr. Theresa Wiseman studied empathy and found it to have the following four qualities:

• Perspective taking,

• Staying out of judgment,

• Recognizing an emotion in another person that you might have felt before, and

• Communicating your recognition and acknowledgment of that emotion.[1]

Empathy is an active joining with a person in their emotional state and validating that experience. It builds connection.

Imagine that your Creative is a budding actor whose dream is to work on Broadway. They have done well—so well, in fact, that they have almost always been cast in significant roles in their high school productions. This time around, they have practiced and worked hard and have decided to audition for their local community theater for the first time—and to go for a part that isn't the obvious one for them in an effort to step outside of their comfort zone. They are ready to listen to those who have told them they need to "go for it," and they have their heart set on a part that may not be the best match for their set of skills, or vocal range, or "type," even though this is their first time auditioning for an adult professional theater and you gently suggested this might not be the time or place to do this, that perhaps they should try for a part that seems more their "type."

And they don't get the part.

Not only are they not cast in the role, they are not cast in *any* named role. They are in the ensemble, a position they have not found themselves in in years. They feel devastated.

There's so much here to unpack—including how great this experience will actually be for their long-term development. (Remember, they haven't been in an ensemble in years —at their age, that means they have developed so many new skills and have dramatically changed what they bring to a performance since their last time being in an ensemble). Maybe you, as a parent, know enough about the industry to understand that learning to excel in an ensemble role is truly part of being a well-rounded musical theater performer—or you know nothing about musical theater, but you know you gently warned your Creative that *even you*, with your lack of knowledge, could see this was the likely outcome in this situation, and you are just thrilled they avoided the potential outcome of not being cast at all.

This is not the time to say, "Oh honey, I know you are disappointed, but this will be so good for your development as an actor and as a person!" Nor is it the time to say, "Wow. Well, I kinda tried to warn you. I didn't think you'd have much of a chance, given who you were up against." Okay, yes, you know that in theory, but in practice, as parents, it's so hard not to fall into grabbing every "teaching" moment when we can, especially with teens and tweens who no longer look to us as the experts on everything and seek out our opinion in their every decision. So even though we *know* this is not what we should do, guess what—we tend to do it to some degree almost reflexively. One dad I spoke with said it very well: "Oh man, I get what you're saying. But it's so hard. I feel like the clock is ticking, and I only have two more years to get all the life lessons in."

This is when we need to dig deep and do some active listening and engage with empathy. Active listening skills are possibly one of the most important parenting skills to figure out. Active listening is focused, respectful, engaged listening. It requires giving your Creative your full attention.

It sounds easy: pay attention, don't interrupt, and ask appropriate, nonjudgmental follow-up questions or offer empathy. When in the throes of parenting, though, this can be so much easier said than done. It means you, as a parent, are not multitasking, looking at a screen, or waiting to give your child your opinion (and boy, do they know when that is what we are doing!).

Why can this be so challenging for us as parents? Well, maybe you are trying to engage in active listening as you hear your Creative offering up excuses with a snarky know-it-all attitude as they explain why the director has it out for them or plays favorites or doesn't know what they are doing (which could actually be true *at the same time* it is true that your Creative didn't make good choices). And maybe you are trying to listen as they imply how little your opinion matters because you are, in fact, not very bright. "Oh Mom, that is so stupid. It doesn't work that way at all!"

Are you still not interrupting? You should get a medal because, man, is this kid out of line now! But you are biting your tongue because you've done your work, you've read your parenting books, and you know that, in this situation, you need to just listen, even if it's taking all you have not to roll your eyes at the ridiculousness of what they are saying. You are patiently waiting and actively listening while trying to swallow back a few follow-up zingers of your own, such as, "Um, so you really thought your first time auditioning in a professional adult theater you should try out for the lead instead of a supporting role?" Or how about "So explain to me again why this well-known regional director is an idiot?"

Active listening can be hard. As a parent, you are listening through a filter of years of life experience, as the person who is funding so many of the opportunities your Creative is exploring, and the person who fears they will be on clean-up duty if it all falls apart for your Creative. But it is so key to building a bridge of trust and understanding with your Creative versus teaching them not to trust you with their emotions around their art.

So you take their perspective, refrain from judgment, identify what emotions they are likely feeling under all of this (Embarrassment? Disappointment? Shame? Fear that they aren't good enough to make a career of this?), relate it to when you have felt those emotions (Remember when you were passed up for a promotion you weren't totally qualified for, but everyone was hyping you up to just go for it?), and sit with your Creative in their emotion. If they have space to hear it, tell them about that time when you felt the same way. Avoid moving from empathy to sympathy. Jump into the heart of the emotion and sit with them there. They will be far more likely to lean toward you as they hear your own expressed vulnerability and understanding, and they will feel supported as they begin to process their emotions.

Sympathy comes from a different place. No one wants to feel pitied. Sympathy feels more like judgment than compassion in many instances. It can create disconnection—"Oh, I'm sorry *you* are feeling so badly. I, on the other hand, am not feeling the same way or even relating to your emotional state because I would know better than to make that mistake—and whew, am I glad I'm not feeling whatever it is you're feeling!"

Dr. Brené Brown said something I have used often in working with parents of Creatives. She said, "Rarely, if ever, does an empathic response begin with 'At least...'" Think about it: "At least you were cast." "At least the role didn't go to another high school student." "At least you will get to learn from people better than you."

It's tempting when someone shares something painful with us—even if they are not verbally calling it pain—to try to make them feel better. For parents, the desire to mitigate our children's pain is almost reflexive. It's also easier for us to avoid being vulnerable ourselves and move into a space of trying to say, "Oh, it's not as bad as you are feeling it to be." This may protect us, but it also invalidates our teen or tween's emotional response. Even though no one enjoys being in pain, it is an inevitable part of life, growth, and learning. You won't help heal the pain by trying to talk them out of their choices or emotions. By connecting with your Creative with empathy, you can help their emotional healing begin faster.

Some examples of useful empathic response statements:

- "You're right."

- "I'm sorry you are dealing with this."

- "I would feel like that too if that happened to me."

- "Let me make sure I understand. You felt like X when Y happened?"

- "This is so hard."

- "I can feel how much you wanted this."

- "This is a really difficult situation to handle."

- "It's really hard when we don't know what is going to happen."

- "I know what it's like to feel like you want to give up. I'm glad you are pushing through."

- "I wish I had been there with you when that happened to you."

When you have shown yourself to be a safe place full of empathy, your Creative is far more likely to share their hopes, dreams, successes, failures, and challenges without fear of judgment.

BE PREPARED FOR EMOTIONAL CATHARSIS

So, you are doing all you can to be the safe place for your Creative to land. You are doing the active listing and empathy thing. You are working hard to model a growth mindset, and you didn't "at least" your Creative in your response. You are a model of the parenting talent (ahem, I mean *skills*) it takes to create the safest, most supportive environment for your Creative. So you are about to reap the loving and respectful rewards of an open and communicative relationship with your Creative... right?

Welp... maybe. But you may also reap the rewards of being the safe place for your Creative to have that emotional meltdown they've held back from having in front of their peers or instructors. Welcome to the world of emotional catharsis.

Have you ever had an utterly frustrating or infuriating encounter with someone with whom you needed to maintain an outward appearance of polite interaction, then come home and furiously vented to your partner or yelled at one of your children over a minor offense that normally wouldn't trigger you? That is emotional catharsis. When you are in the presence of the emotional safety of your most secure relationships, you can dump all of that pent-up negative emotion you were holding in.

Because you have done all of the hard work to be your teen or tween's safe place, they are more likely to lash out full force at you than anywhere else when they've had a bad day.

Congratulations.

No, really, it is a good thing. It's a sign of a developing ability to emotionally regulate when it is necessary—to not impulsively react in anger in the moment, to not say something inappropriate or something that would escalate a situation. Your Creative managed it until they were safely with you.

This catharsis may also happen in the form of crying. It may look like a disproportionate reaction to a situation where your teen or tween starts crying and can't stop. They may even be bewildered by their response, saying, "I don't know why I'm crying about this." Reassure them that it is normal for that to happen occasionally and the crying is letting out all of the frustration, sadness, or anger that has built up about many things.

When emotional catharsis happens, try to let the emotion run its course while staying calm—or, if your teen or tween is crying, by providing comfort. This can be a silent hug. In fact, not saying anything is usually better than trying to make them feel better. Then, when the moment has passed, give them some time to regroup and then suggest that you process what they were feeling together—even if it's just to let them know you'd appreciate a statement such as "Sorry, I was mad about something else and I overreacted when you asked me to put my camera equipment away." Oh, and remember—when you have your own emotional catharsis that lands on them, model the same. "I'm sorry. My reaction wasn't about you."

TAKE CARE OF YOURSELF AND AVOID PARENTING RAGE

We're all just trying to do the best we can here—right? We all have moments where our best is marginal, especially if we aren't taking care of ourselves.

Self-care is imperative to being a good parent. If we are neglecting our own needs, or feeling burned out, unseen, or unsupported, we simply cannot meet others' needs effectively.

Self-care is essential for stress relief and overall wellness. As parents, we tend to constantly put the needs of our kids well before our own. Finding the time or resources for self-care often falls to the bottom of our priority list, and this type of self-neglect will only lead to decreased parenting skills.

Even small acts of self-care can go far in helping us shore up our own emotional and physical reserves. Perhaps this looks like choosing to walk to purchase a coffee after a rough morning instead of making one at home. Or, at home, it might look like splurging on your favorite brand of coffee (or wine) once a month.

Prioritize sleep and other types of restorative time—yoga, meditation, reading a book uninterrupted at a coffee house, watching a show, taking yourself to a movie midday—whatever works for you.

Learn to delegate. Sometimes, as parents, we feel it's just easier to take care of things ourselves, but if we are always the ones in charge of all the things, there is often little time for downtime. Downtime is something I see so many parents struggle with. They feel guilty if they are doing "nothing" or if they take time for a quick nap. Yet, when they do, they can admit that they experience their days as less stressful.

Parental rage is a very real thing. When we are not taking care of ourselves, we are much more likely to find ourselves yelling. Rage happens when our anger or frustration boils over in uncontrolled outbursts. We are far more likely to have an outburst of rage when two things are happening: when we are feeling depleted (which can come from a lack of self-care) or when we aren't aware of our triggers.

Learning to tune in to when you feel parental rage will help you avoid those not-so-proud moments when you lose it and find yourself screaming, "No! I cannot bring you your camera bag—I told you a thousand times to put it by your backpack last night! I don't care if you were supposed to shoot the game today. Borrow one from school!" When parents are feeling burned out, I ask them to start making a quick note on their phone of what is going on any time they feel rage bubbling to the surface. Usually it does not take long for them to figure out what some of their biggest triggers are, which allows us to engage in some preventive planning. Here are some examples.

• Is your trigger an action, such as last-minute requests that interrupt your schedule? Talk to your Creative ahead of time and let them know this is something you can no longer accommodate. If they are open to it, brainstorm what they can do from their end to decrease or stop such requests.

• Is your trigger the feeling that money is being wasted? Again, have a conversation with your Creative when you are feeling calm and explain why this is a trigger for you. Often, just knowing where a parent is coming from can create a change in behavior from a teen or tween.

• Is your trigger an emotional situation, such as events that remind you of the death of a parent? Try to anticipate when this may come up, like at a holiday concert when you see other Creatives' grandparents in the audience cheering them on. Sometimes just recognizing your increased sensitivity can help you keep the misplaced rage under control.

Creative beings are often very temperamentally perceptive in addition to being sensitive, and they may internalize rage outbursts from you in a very deep way. The best way to avoid this is to avoid the rage outbursts to begin with. But we are all imperfect, and if and when you do find yourself realizing you had a momentary rage response, take a breath, apologize, and talk to your Creative about what was going on inside. Model taking responsibility for your actions and emotions.

If you find yourself in a pattern of parental rage, get some outside help.

IMPLEMENTATION

When things are rough, taking a step back and looking at the behavior from a different perspective may help you shift your interactions with your Creative to a more outwardly loving expression. Are you able to look at the situation with a growth mindset and point out the success and learning that did take place, even if the outcome was not entirely what was desired? Are you able to see where perfectionism or vulnerability may have led to paralysis around actions that would have prevented the outcome? I often find that taking a beat before responding to my kids' big emotions helps me engage in a more constructive manner than I would have if I just jumped in reflexively.

I know, personally, I once had a hard time dealing with my son's inconsistency in his practice routine. But once I shifted my thinking about his consistency (or lack thereof) in the context of learning styles, my way of relating to him changed. I was able to let go of my much more comfortable (and, let's be honest, in my mind, logical—because doesn't everyone approach the world this way?) linear approach and look at the big picture. Was he accomplishing his goals (versus mine)? At times when the answer was yes—when his teachers commented on his progress, his musical thought process, and how he came in with interesting questions—then I had to assume that his way was working. At times when the answer was no, I was better able to calmly discuss with him what he and I could do to help him make changes that avoided the problem in the future.

Did this always work? Heck no. Plenty of days I would see his piano book lying where he had left it after his last lesson, gathering dust while he was "practicing" daily. His definition of practicing was doing what he considered the fun part of piano. He has a natural ear and can pick up chords and general melodies easily. Thus, it was, of course, infinitely more fun for him to sing and accompany himself. Working to shore up his note-reading, on the other hand, was not enjoyable for him. I won't pretend that there aren't days when I have given him a mom glare as I handed him his book and asked him to *please* spend at least ten minutes of his practice time on the actual assigned tasks.

But I also noticed that, over time, because I had shifted my approach and given him more room to process and proceed the way that worked best for him, he was more receptive to my—*ahem*—gentle suggestions. He noticed I wasn't on top of him for every practice session, while I noticed he was more receptive to addressing things I inquired about. It made the entire journey more pleasant for us both (most of the time).

Chapter 12

Two Extremes—Moving Up and Moving On

WHEN YOUR CREATIVE WANTS TO GO PRO

My husband and I both have advanced degrees. We grew up in an era where the message was "College or perish on minimum wage." I didn't give it much thought. I'd assumed my kids would go to a competitive college or university just like we had.

T is the third of four kids and he, well, he just did not care about grades the way the others did. He had A's and B's, but also quite a few C's, which in our home used to mean consequences and tutoring. But T only really cared about two things: his bass and making music. He's a good kid in all other ways—kind, helpful, really good with younger kids, respectful—he just did not care about school.

He had a great work ethic in many ways—around music, of course, but also around his summer jobs. We had to really take a step back and think about what was important. Did we want a kid who was angry and stressed and resentful and sad and frustrated but who had straight A's, or did we want a happy, pleasant, fulfilled kid who was pursuing his passion? So we backed off and told him that as long as he pulled off a 2.5 for each semester, we would leave him alone.

I won't lie, I was a bit terrified. But he really seemed to flourish once the pressure was off. He began working on a music portfolio, learned upright bass, was gigging quite a bit, and developed an EPK [Electronic Press Kit], a term I'd never heard before he started using it.

When it came time to apply for school, it turned out he'd done his research and he was ready. He'd been working with his bass instructor to prepare for his auditions, and he came to us with a mix of schools ranging from highly academically competitive with sought after music programs to more lax scholastic requirements but highly competitive on the music side. I had to have my friends talk me off the edge and let him do his thing, but in the end, guess what? He wound up with a 3.0 GPA and he chose a decently academically rigorous school with a highly regarded contemporary music program. When he [told us his decision], we sat him down and told him that if he wanted to go to what he used to call his dream school—a contemporary music school—we would support him. He said he'd thought about it, and it wasn't that he didn't care about the other parts of education, but he just cared about music more, and he thought that the school he chose was the best balance. I was so relieved.

It turns out that, even though he did well and maintained decent grades in college, he excelled in the music department and in the greater music community. He decided to take a hiatus for one year in good standing and started touring with an up-and-coming singer who'd attended his school. We had to let go—he's an adult. And to be honest, he's only asked for money once, and he offered to pay it back. So he made the right choice for himself, and he already has another tour with another artist lined up and has told us that at this point, he doesn't see himself going back to college in the foreseeable future.

We've all heard the phrase "starving artist." As parents, the one thing we don't want to think about is our adult children struggling to make it. We didn't sacrifice over and over to set them up for "success" because we have no investment in the outcome. We want them to have financial security—and it can be concerning when our children make choices that, from your perspective, may not have a clear path to job security and decent pay.

Yet the world needs the arts. When the world shut down unexpectedly during the COVID-19 pandemic, our isolation quickly demonstrated why humans are drawn to the arts. The arts build community and common cultural experiences. They promote connection and social interaction. They can provide comfort, strength, and a sense of being seen, understood, and valued and are an expression of what it means to be human.

A desire to make a living from one's passion is understandable and desirable in many ways. So what is a parent to do when their teen or tween says, "This isn't a hobby. This is my future career."?

SUPPORT THEIR PASSION

If you are fully on board and accepting—or even celebrating—this news, then supporting your Creative's desire to take their art to the next level should be an easy transition. Ask questions about when and why they made this choice and what you can do to help. Encourage them to do plenty of research and know what path they want to explore to turn their art into a career and what they may need to do in the interim to ensure they are prepared to either apply to a school or training program or become an entrepreneur.

If you are struggling with, ambivalent about, or vehemently against this decision, this is absolutely not the moment to back away from that support. At the very least, doing so can be confusing. Think of it from your Creative's perspective. Their parent has always been the one to help them find and pay for training, to be in the front row of all of their performances, to post their artwork on social media, to encourage others to look at their product, and to brag to others about their increasing skills. Now that they want to take that to a new level, you are invalidating the time, energy, and skill development they have spent on this endeavor and are discouraging them from this next—what may seem completely logical to them—step in their passion.

As parents, it can be hard to avoid letting judgment sneak into our conversations with our teens. One of the easiest ways to limit this is to use those active listening skills you developed when offering empathy and to listen to what they have to say. Ask leading but open-ended questions like the following:

- When did you decide this was the path you wanted to take?

- How did you come to this decision?

- Have you done any research yet?

Nod and listen, and only comment when your Creative asks you to do so, but keep things as neutral as possible, letting them know you are gathering information so you can offer the best support once you understand the variables. This is their current decision; they need space to own that and figure things out in their own way without judgment.

On a more serious level, if you express judgment, that judgment can create identity issues, make your teen feel incompetent to make decisions, and make your teen question both their skill level and your belief in their skill level. To suddenly shift gears and imply in any way that their investment is not legitimate can be a crushing blow and can cause a rift in the parent-teen relationship. Take a beat to process their desire—and, in the meantime, keep being their biggest cheerleader as you figure out the best next steps and an appropriate and supportive way to hear and discuss the "how" and "why" of the desire.

Be prepared. Their version of what their future career might look like and how they plan to get there may be incredibly different from what you'd hoped or dreamed for them. Keep the lines of communication open and begin talking about goals, dreams, training, and sustainable income.

BE AUTHENTIC IN YOUR SUPPORT

If your teen is interested in pursuing their art as their career, you need to take in their intention and show up authentically to support them. If you aren't on board with this career choice, but instead of showing up authentically, you pretend you are happy (or at least nonresistant), your teen will instantly sense your dishonesty and resistance. If you know this is you and you want to keep the lines of communication and trust open, you will need to take a step back and find a part of what your teen is saying that you can connect with. Can you connect with the fact that they are starting to think about their future? Then focus on that part —and respond accordingly. Are you impressed by the research they did before approaching you? Show your excitement about their maturity there. And, like we talked about in chapter 11, try your best to avoid "but" statements, as most of us have experienced how quickly those invalidate a response.

If you want to be authentically supportive but you are struggling with the decision and the words aren't coming easily just yet, demonstrate continued authentic support in your actions. Do things that support and deepen your Creative's exploration of their art. Offer to look for (and, if they are open to it, to join your Creative in attending) free or paid events featuring professionals in their art of choice. Attending art shows, dance performances, music concerts, digital/content creator conventions, workshops, and master-classes shows authentic support and helps both you and your Creative explore more of what it would mean for them to be a professional in their art of choice. You may also offer to help them find new resources and discuss any additional tools or equipment they may feel will help them and how to obtain those resources within the family budget. It's always good to look for and ask for scholarships to programs you may not be able to afford. There may also be local resources available to assist with material goods needed for your Creative's art career exploration.

I can't lie—I really struggled a bit with G's choice to pursue being an artist. But it forced me to really think about what messages I want her to get from us—and one was "be your authentic self." So the one thing I could honestly say was that I knew G was at her happiest when she was creating— drawing, painting, whatever. That's when she is both calm and lit up all at once. So I just tried to focus on that messag- ing. "I know art is what makes you happy." And I backed off the other stuff until I was ready to really be supportive and not be coming at her from a place of fear. Because I didn't want to undermine her feelings about being an artist—I want her to keep her happiness around it. I just kept telling myself, "It's her authentic self, and I'm proud of her for sticking to that."

What's funny is that she said "artist" and I didn't even really have a good conversation with her for a while because I was worried she would sense I wasn't fully on board. When we did talk to her, she said she was really thinking about becoming an art therapist. She loved working with the kids in the studio she worked for, and she really loved helping them express emotions they didn't have words for. I had had no idea. So she was saying "studio arts major," but she had a bigger plan past that. And that's what she's doing. She's in a master's program now for art therapy, and she loves it. It fits who she is perfectly.

ACKNOWLEDGE YOUR OWN FEARS

Having your teen or tween say "I want to be an artist" can be terrifying, especially if you have limited experience with people who have made successful careers in the arts. If you cannot relate to this sentiment and you are overjoyed that your kid is turning their passion into their career, feel free to skip to the last section in this chapter, "Discuss Entrepreneurial Lessons for Older Teens." But if you are fighting an urge to scream "Where have we gone wrong? There is no way they can survive as an artist!" then the next two sections are for you.

It's important to acknowledge and process any anxiety, fear, or misgivings you have about your child's desire to turn their artistic passion into a career. Unfortunately, some around you may only serve to feed your fears. "Oh, an [insert creative career of choice here]? That's so great! *[Insert high-pitched fake tone.]* How do you feel about that? *[Insert pitying look.]* I don't think that would be a good choice for my kid. We've decided a more practical career makes more sense for them. *[Insert slightly superior tone]*." Supporting your Creative's choice can sometimes feel like a lonely and misguided journey.

We live in a society that, for many years, has defined a "successful" conclusion to high school to be matriculation into a four-year school with a "practical" major with an allegedly clearly defined career path. Though times are changing, and more and more students are taking a step back to reconsider this pathway, it can still be scary—and yes, for some, embarrassing—when our children don't conform to the implied definition of a safe path.

Acknowledging any fears you have around this choice is essential for keeping the lines of communication open between you and your Creative and supporting them. More than once, I've had to explain to a teary teen client that fear is often expressed as anger, and their parents' initial angry or disappointed response may be coming from a place of unacknowledged or unresolved fear—which comes from a place of loving them. Yet it will not feel like love to your Creative if your response is tinged with sarcasm, anger, disappointment, or any other negative emotion.

If you find yourself stuck in negative emotions around your Creative's career aspirations, it may be time to get some outside support. There is no one right path to happiness, and if your teen is saying they need to explore a path you have reservations about helping them traverse, remind yourself that the goal is to raise your child to be a unique, fulfilled, independent adult. It may not be the easiest path, but the grit, determination, and resilience your Creative has learned in development of the skills in their art will come into play and help them figure out their own unique journey.

EXPRESS ANY CONCERNS IN AN EMOTIONALLY SAFE MANNER

This is, of course, the best approach in any conversation with your teen—but for potentially sensitive topics, it is even more important to create a safe space where your teen feels they are respected and their thought process and opinions are valued. Take a moment to first think about where your concerns are coming from. Are you fearful your Creative won't be able to make a living? Are you secretly thinking they don't have a high enough skill level to make it professionally or be accepted into a program that focuses on their art? Do you worry that their art of choice is a challenging way to make a living, or do you have no idea how to guide them toward doing so? Are you concerned that they may want to begin working in their art immediately instead of going to school for it first? Are you feeling anxiety about the cost of pursuing an education in their art? Do you fear that, though they have skills in their art, they don't have the necessary business skills to become an entrepreneur?

Once you have gotten in touch with your underlying concern(s), you will be better prepared to have a constructive conversation with your Creative without triggering defensiveness in either of you. Your Creative is far more likely to be receptive to your concerns when they're phrased as "I" statements—"I'm concerned about your long-term prospects to support yourself, and I would appreciate it if you would tell me more about how people make a living doing X" is a much more engaging conversation-starter than "There is no way you are going to be able to support yourself, so you'd better have a plan."

Think ahead to determine when it might be best to have this conversation. When will you both be rested and ready to process what the other person is saying? If your teen is the type to open up much more when riding in a car with you (thus limiting eye contact), plan an errand that creates a decent amount of time to talk. If your teen tends to open up at night after the house has settled down, initiate the conversation on an evening when you know you will have plenty of time and no pressure about getting up early the next day. How will you respond to your teen if they say something you do not agree with? How will you keep your tone neutral and your questions open? Are you prepared to temporarily shelve the conversation if you find yourself becoming worked up? Most importantly, are you able to remind yourself that this conversation is about your love for and concern about your teen—not about control? By creating an emotionally safe environment for your teen, you are creating a space for better communication and deeper connection.

Hear your teen out. Even if they don't have all of the answers, create a conversation that makes them want to seek out those answers and share them with you rather than shutting down and feeling dejected.

ENCOURAGE SELF-DISCOVERY

If your Creative is expressing true interest in creating a career with their art, then helping them develop a deeper understanding of who they are in relation to their art will help set them up for success. Some concepts to consider and discuss with them as they explore what path they want to engage in as they develop a career plan:

• How do you work best? In a group? Alone? With deadlines? Without? In a quiet environment?

• How do you learn best? Traditional school model? Project-based learning?

• What motivates you?

• What are your emotional strengths and weaknesses, and how do they influence your art?

• What about your art makes you happy? What about your art do you find challenging?

• Where do you want to be in six months? A year? Five years?

• What is the biggest dream you have for your art if every single possible thing goes right?

• Are there any aspects of your art that you would rather *not* incorporate into your future career?

As a parent, you can model what it looks like to engage in life and career exploration, commitment, and reflection. Talk about your own choices and how you came to those. How did you work through the hard parts of your career? What did you do when things were tough as you were working your way up in your career? How did you know when it was time to shift gears? What did that feel like, and how did you go about it? Relate these themes back to your teen's choices and challenges in their education and art to date and encourage them to think about what this may look like once they commit to their art as their career.

If you feel your experiences aren't applicable or you are uncomfortable advising them on career matters connected to their art, there are other resources available. Encourage them to reach out to other adults who have worked in the field and read bibliographies and biographies about artists they admire or might want to emulate, or suggest other media resources such as podcasts or even YouTube videos. Information and support are much more accessible nowadays than they were twenty years ago. Encourage your Creative to take advantage of the bounty at their fingertips.

EDUCATE YOURSELF

If you yourself are not an artist in the same creative space as your teen, chances are you may have a limited understanding of the pathways to success in that area. If you are not involved in the arts—or their specific art—you may find that your concept of what is important, why it is important, and how to get there might not align with the experience of those in the industry themselves. For example, being a "visual artist" is not limited to showing art in galleries or making commissioned pieces. That is just one small part of a vast array of careers and opportunities for someone who works in the visual arts.

If you are able, see if you can find your own mentor or coach who can help you navigate your Creative's journey to a sustainable-income career path in their art. No two paths are the same, and there are so many variables to consider that it can be a bit overwhelming if you are having to step outside not only your comfort zone but also your experience zone, as you learn to better support your teen. A mentor or coach who is experienced in your Creative's art or in helping Creative's navigate different career paths can be invaluable to both you and your teen. Many parents I've spoken to have said that, while it was truly well intentioned, the advice their Creatives received from their high school career counselor was not specifically accurate for their chosen career paths. Seek advice from someone who understands the ins and outs of the options.

Mentors do not necessarily need to be prominent figures

in your Creative's art—though, of course, if you have access to that, absolutely take advantage of that connection. However, sometimes other artists only a few years ahead of your Creative may have the most relevant and applicable advice. Mentors can be current or former instructors, educators in the career of choice, or people you locate on social media. Again, our world is so much larger than it was in the past; you have the opportunity to ask for guidance from people around the world. Not everyone will be open to helping you out, but when you ask, you may be surprised by how many are open to—or even excited about—the idea of offering guidance to a parent who is supporting their Creative's love for their art.

What does "success" look like in your Creative's art? "Fame" is not the definition of success in the arts. Those who are famous represent a very small portion of those who practice a given form of art. The majority of adult Creatives managing successful careers in their arts of choice are not known, are only known locally, or have some degree of recognition in certain circles within their art but no name or face recognition in the general population. Find out what your Creative defines as success and engage in conversations about what it will mean to have a sustainable income, sustainable income being income they can count on coming in consistently and meeting the needs of their monthly budget.

Once you have a good sense of what your Creative is hoping to manifest as a career in their art, educate yourself as to how others have gotten to where your Creative hopes to be. Did most go to four-year colleges? Did they major in the art, or did they choose another skill to focus on as a sustainable income source? For some, this may come from within or closely adjacent to their art such as moonlighting as an instructor at an after-school art program. For others, they may choose something completely unrelated but still affords them time to pursue their art. Did they go to an alternative training program (like a two-year program or a shorter specialized program), or did they choose not to attend a formal program at all? Will your Creative need or benefit from an internship? If your Creative indicates that they plan on going to school for a career path that is not directly aligned with the skills needed for their desired career outcome—such as a musician who is considering a music education degree, even though their ultimate goal is to be a contemporary songwriter—then I'd encourage a deep dive into why they are considering this and whether it will truly serve their career goals. If not, then it may be time for some additional exploration and education. What are the skills your Creative truly needs to put their dreams in reach?

D has always wanted to be an artist. That was the dream. I never really had a good sense of what she would do for money, you know? Like, unless you are a commissioned artist, how do you make a living?

We really started pushing her to get a four-year degree to fall back on. She resisted, but eventually she said she would major in education so she could be an elementary art teacher and paint on the side.

The summer after her junior year of high school, she went to camp and, on the last day, they had a showcase in the afternoon, but in the morning, while the kids were packing up and saying their goodbyes, they had parent seminars. One was on "life after high school." It was like the lecturer had been listening to our conversations. She talked about how much pressure she had felt to go to school because it was what her parents had wanted.

As the lecturer spoke, my husband and I looked at one another. We knew D didn't really have a passion for teaching at all; she was just moving into the path of least resistance. On the long drive home, we had a very different conversation with her, and we really tried to just listen. Ultimately, we all agreed that spending that kind of money for a field she was never going to enjoy made no sense. Instead, for now D is pursuing an art and design certificate, and she started an online business. She's doing well, already making money. She's living at home, and her plan is to save all her earnings so she can purchase a condo in the future and keep building her online business. She's now said she may go to school for her bachelor's at some point, but if she does, it would be as a business major to help her build her business.

BACK OFF STRAIGHT A'S

I think also academically some of the things I pushed N about—grades, certain classes—didn't really matter in the end. Perhaps taking some of those classes pushed him creatively? I don't know. I think I would have done things differently, let go of some things about school and grades and used that time and energy on other things, if I'd known where he was going to land [majoring in contemporary music]. Shoulda, woulda, coulda... ultimately, he's in a pretty good place.

Yeah, I know. I heard your gasp. I really do get it, especially if you were a conscientious student and feel traditional education is the best path to a *career* rather than a *job*. But hear me out.

Teens and tweens today are under so much pressure. There are so many expectations on them. High school looks very different now than it did in the past. Where the top students may have taken mostly honors classes or maybe two

AP-level classes during their senior years back in the day, nowadays the top students need to be taking at least a few APs by sophomore year and often five APs by junior year.

The homework volume for this type of academic rigor is daunting. High school students often tell me they consider four hours of homework a "light" amount. If your Creative is working to develop high-level career-making skills in their art, this may already be taking up two to four hours of after-school time before they even consider touching their academic work. Exhaustion and burnout are very real threats, and, depending on your Creative's goals, the trade-off may not be worth it.

Is your Creative a writer who is aiming to attend an Ivy League school or other highly competitive institution? In that case, a very real conversation about where they should place their primary focus makes sense. And for them, it likely makes sense to aim for straight A's in the most rigorous English and writing classes their high school offers and pair those classes with other APs.

Is your Creative looking for admission to a highly academically competitive school where they can major in their art? Make sure they know both the general academic requirements for admission and the specific admission requirements for their program of choice and plan accordingly. Are they managing their academics and still finding enough time to progress in their art outside of academics? Look at how to support them best in a way that fits their goals. For example, they may need gentle reminders to plan ahead, look at the calendar, and consider backing out in advance of a recital, show, or exhibition that falls in the middle of finals.

If a top-tier, highly academically competitive school is not your Creative's goal, then it may be time to take a step back and make sure the primary place their energy is going is in alignment with their goals. Does it make more sense for them to drop a few AP-level classes in subjects they have no interest in studying? Is a reading- and writing-heavy AP History course truly necessary for their goals? If their goal is college, but they aren't sure where, again, take a look at the current admissions requirements for your state schools that offer the majors your Creative has expressed an interest in pursuing. Talk to your Creative. Watch for signs of how well they are managing all of the demands currently placed on them and how that matches with their goals. Maybe straight A's are manageable if your Creative pulls back from the most rigorous track for a few of their classes, and doing so will serve them better for admission to the right program. Look at what will truly impact their chances of success in the programs or pathway they are most interested in.

This does not in any way mean you need to abandon all expectations for their academic performance or work ethic. It's about being open to taking a step back and deciding where that rigor and work ethic are best prioritized. Talk to your Creative and explain your thinking and expectations. If your Creative is adamant that they are not looking to go to college, but the option of a traditional four-year school is important to you, discuss what it would take to at least keep the option of college open and consider coming to a relevant compromise. Learning high standards and a work ethic in any area will develop traits that will apply to many areas of your Creative's life.

Another important concept to consider: to obtain straight A's, a student must conform to a very specific and limited set of expectations. There is little or no room for true creativity in how that is achieved. Straight-A students are typically very good at memorizing and synthesizing information and spitting it back out on structured tests, but obtaining straight A's is often not a measure of the ability to engage in teamwork, leadership, or creativity—all of which are important skills in many arts.

In order to have a successful career in the arts, originality is typically highly valued and sought after. Thinking outside the box and approaching tasks in a new way may be some of the most important skill sets for your Creative to focus on in their time away from academics. The more time they have to explore and develop those skills, the more prepared they may be to pursue and succeed in the career they desire.

ACKNOWLEDGE THAT IT'S THEIR LIFE

One of the best and most powerful things you can do for your teen is to let them know that you believe in their ability to make their own decisions. It's their life, and they have to be the one in charge of what direction it takes. On the other hand, one of the fastest ways to undermine your relationship is to invalidate their thought process and the path that it leads them down.

As a parent, your final hands-on task is to launch your Creative into the world prepared to live the life they choose to live. You may not agree with their choice, you may lament many parts of it, and you may be struggling in these early steps of your Creative's full independence from you, but a quick way to build resentment between you and your teen is to put them in a position of having to choose between living their own truth and living with your disapproval. You may win the battle, but you will not win the war. Whether the loss is in the form of them bending to your will and resenting your control or rejecting your will and feeling alienated, there is no good outcome in either direction.

Your teen's developmental job is to move toward independence. If this independence does not fit in with the life you had hoped and dreamed of for them, it may be challenging or even painful for you to shift your dream to their dream. Holding on tightly to our teens may make us feel good and may give us the illusion of control, but that is all it is—an illusion. By acknowledging your Creative's hopes and dreams and finding a way to engage with them as a young adult who is now ready to create their own path, you are offering them the greatest gift you can: stepping aside and letting them know that you trust their ability to stand on their own and manage their own choices. This is the surest way to encourage your teen to see you as a trusted resource for advice, support, and comfort when they hit bumps in the road.

If you are struggling to be open-minded and supportive, try to at least not be negative about your teen's decision to pursue a creative arts career. Set boundaries for yourself around what topics you are open to discussing and which ones to avoid. Focus on the relationship you want with your grown child—do you want one that is based in mutual respect, admiration, and friendship, or one that is rife with stress, mistrust, and disrespect? Assuming the vast majority of parents truly want the former, take a step back and ask yourself how you can go about building that. Undermining your teen's hopes, dreams, and identity as an artist is counterproductive.

So, you know what's hard? Realizing you are not the parent you told yourself you were. Because had you asked me five years ago, I'd say I was a super supportive "go get your dream" kind of parent. Turns out, that was because my older two had dreams that lined up with my vision of their future. My oldest? Wanted to go into premed. My middle? Biotech.

The baby, T, is eleven years younger than her siblings. She was a truly happy surprise. Always bubbly and easygoing and creative, but she never really liked school much. She came along after all of this social media was exploding. So I never dealt with it with my older two.

I was pretty naive. When she was in middle school, T asked if she was allowed to post YouTube videos, and I said, "Sure!" without much thought. Same thing when she mentioned that she could make some money if she let ads run on her channel and asked if I would be okay with that. I said sure again and helped her fill out the forms and bank information and watched a few videos. They were cute, but I just didn't really get it, you know?

It was my middle child who, four years later, said, "You know, T has a pretty big following on YouTube." What? So I hopped on and found out she was what I now know is called an "influencer." She did makeup and skin-care videos. I knew at one point she had babysat primarily to make money for makeup, but I just never really focused on why. Long story short, she started making some decent money right around when she turned sixteen, and shortly after that, she came to me and said her schedule was too busy and she either wanted me to homeschool her or she was seriously considering dropping out.

Bye-bye, happy-go-lucky "follow your dream" mom. I lost it. And my peers—yeah, they just fed into it. Lots of "She what? Oh, I'm so sorry. Can't you just forbid her to go on YouTube?"

It was my oldest who got through to me. She flew in to mediate—or so I thought. Now I see it was to take up her sister's cause. But she showed me numbers, articles, and all sorts of things to say, "Mom, this is a thing, and she's actually doing really well at it, and right now she's on track to make more than me." So I agreed T could homeschool as long as she found and paid for a formal online program, instead of having me trying to figure that out this late in the game. And she did it. She found a program that fit my criteria but also allowed her to move at her own pace, and she actually managed to graduate a semester early. She's smart, and I had to let her use her smarts her way, not mine. And she's doing great. She doesn't want to be on YouTube forever, so she's taken her savings and has invested and is talking about starting another online business.

ENTREPRENEURIAL LESSONS TO DISCUSS WITH OLDER TEENS

If your Creative is pursuing their art as a career, there is a very good chance they will spend some—if not all—of their time as an entrepreneur.

Creatives don't always see their choice to work as an artist as becoming an entrepreneur. Yet, if a life in the arts is the route they are choosing, it will be very beneficial to help them understand that success may very well mean being a solopreneur or a small business entrepreneur. Even if their chosen path to their art includes a four-year degree, this does not necessarily mean they will have been taught the basic entrepreneurial lessons they will need to create the careers they desire within their art.

There are many skills they will need to develop in order to become self-sufficient within their creative art. Encourage your Creative to have a solid understanding of the skills they will need to move forward and learn how to obtain the ones they may not have yet or may not be very strong in.

A few skills you may want to discuss with your teen that, at the very least, may be beneficial and in some cases may even be essential include:

• Self-reliance

• Business accounting

- Principles of marketing

- Digital and social media marketing

- Customer service

- Teamwork and leadership

- Communication (this includes, yes, actually checking their email)

- Business strategy

- Efficiency and productivity

- Networking

- Hiring and training

- Basic SEO

- Finding and closing leads

- Taking responsibility for end results

If you have some or many of these skills and can share them with your Creative (and if your Creative is open to that), then wonderful. If you are like many of us who may find some or all of this list a little daunting or aren't sure where to begin, there are many resources available to address skill building in these areas. For many, one of the most accessible and economical resources is the local community college. Community colleges often have classes addressing these skills as well as certificate programs that include multiple skill sets in a single program. If getting your Creative involved at your local community college is not an option for you, do a search for "small business workshops." Many communities have small business resources that include free or low-cost in-person classes or webinars, courses on demand, and content libraries, and these may prove to be a great starting point. There are also many online programs, both created by formal institutions or by other solopreneurs, that may be extremely beneficial.

> We're not a "you must go to college" family. Neither me nor my husband went to college—he's a plumber and I have a medical billing certificate that allows me to work with lots of flexibility because we knew we wanted four kids and I wanted to be a stay-at-home mom. We live in a town where the majority of people do have college degrees, but we can afford to live here because my husband is very successful in his trade and owns his own business, and we didn't have student loans to pay off. We lived frugally for a few years in a one-bedroom apartment in a kind of sketchy area, but we saved a ton and bought our house before we had our first child.
>
> So when K said she wanted to skip college and figure out how to make money with her paintings, we were fine with that. Her summer job had always been working for my husband, so we knew she has a great work ethic, and she also knows what it means to own a small business.
>
> So we sat down and talked about our expectations for her to live with us rent-free while she built her business. We also asked her to submit a "business plan" to us with short- and long-term goals. She had a plan and opened an online shop with merchandise featuring her art even before she finished her senior year. She's into a lot of that new age stuff, and her art is big and colorful and reflects that.

She had a plan. She started selling online in a few places, but her goal was to have her own web store and send traffic there. She researched and asked for money for training programs to help her learn SEO, Etsy, Pinterest, blogging, and online sales. She used the money she made to invest in an ads course and then used her earnings to run ads. We're really, really proud of her, and she's happy because she can spend half of her time painting and half of her time running the business side.

She's branched out into other areas and has gotten a few commissions from people who love her merchandise. She called a mentor to ask how to price those and, though she felt she was asking too much, she now realizes that the first commission probably would have paid more if she'd asked. She's talked about moving out, but she uses our heated garage as her studio, so now she's thinking she's going to try to wait to save enough to get a starter house.

Whether your Creative's desire to turn their passion into a career thrills or terrifies you, this is an amazing time in their life. Launching into adulthood is a natural developmental transition. If your Creative knows their parent has their back, supports them, and will be there cheering them on as they are emerging into adulthood, you will be offering them the best foundation you can as they find their way.

WHEN YOUR CREATIVE SAYS THEY WANT TO QUIT

There may come a time after what some parents may suggest included years of blood, sweat, and tears invested in their art when a Creative decides they are no longer interested in or as passionate about their craft. The decision to let go of something they potentially spent countless hours enjoying, developing, and sharing might be truly painful for all involved, but hard decisions may need to be made if your Creative is telling you that they are no longer invested in their art. That said, there are some things you may want to consider before your Creative walks away from their art.

Do a Well-Being Check

Is there something serious going on that you may not be aware of? No matter how much we may think we know about what is going on in our children's lives, their developmental job is to increasingly demonstrate independence from us. In spite of your best efforts, constant check-ins, and open communication, there may be reasons you aren't aware of that have made continuing in their art untenable. Some questions to consider about your Creative's well-being include the following:

• Are they feeling tremendous stress or anxiety?

• Is there a mental health issue that is interfering with their energy or their ability to focus on their art?

• Is there some type of toxicity in the environment around their art, or is there some other emotional pain connected to the activity?

• Has something shifted that has changed their art from something that causes them joy to something unhealthy?

• Is something damaging their spirit or causing them to question their self-worth?

• Is there a physical issue they have downplayed (in spite of your checking in) that is now becoming too much for them to manage?

Try to Discover the "Why"

If there is no larger well-being issue fueling your Creative's desire to quit their art, it makes sense to want to understand what is behind the shift. This is especially true if you are surprised by this turn of events.

Here are some questions that can help you identify your Creative's "why."

• Are they feeling stuck?

• Do they not feel their instructor or class is a good match, or do they feel that they've outgrown them?

• Are they feeling left out if their friends are doing something else?

• Is the time demand too much? Are they beginning to feel they can no longer progress while meeting the demands of other responsibilities or interests?

• Has it become too competitive for their liking?

• Do they feel as though they have lost their ownership of their art, meeting the expectations and demands of instructors or teams but not their own desires?

• Is there a social issue—do they not get along with someone who is in their art space?

• If they are on a team or in a group of some sort, are they feeling they aren't valued or they don't get many opportunities to shine?

• Are they burned out and just craving a break—perhaps a temporary one?

Once you have a better understanding of what is behind the reason for the shift away from their art, you can work with them to see if quitting is what they really want. Do they just need a break or a break from the skill-building aspect, or are they in fact ready to move on?

Engage in Introspection

It's also important to look at your own motivation if you are tempted to actively discourage your Creative from quitting. This is especially true if they have a well-thought-out reason for wanting to quit—even if you may not fully agree with that reason.

Are you pushing them to keep going because they've always been active in this art? Are you sad because it's something you wanted to do yourself but weren't able to because you didn't have the support you are giving your child? Do you feel like they need to have a set focus on an activity because their siblings all have one? Are you worried they will "lose ground" and have a hard time catching back up if they decide to return to their art at a later date? Had you hoped that their art would become an avenue to scholarships for college or that it would become their major? Are you simply feeling emotional as you think about how you will miss participating in their art as a spectator?

If the opposite is true—as in, your Creative said "quit" and you found yourself trying to suppress a squeal of joy—just be sure that your Creative's wish to move on isn't a response to any unspoken pressure from *you*. Without meaning to, you might have been giving off signals that you were ready for a change. Whether you were making comments about being tired of doing late-night pickups from rehearsals, frequently sharing observations on the exorbitant cost of lessons, supplies, competitions, and other related expenditures, or reflecting about the excessive time commitment and how it impacts your family, you may have been giving your Creative tacit encouragement to quit. Make sure they are truly ready to move on—and if you are convinced they are, in fact, ready to let their art go for their own reasons, then try to wait until you're in private before you do your happy dance.

Take a Beat

When your teen or tween asks to quit, unless there is an urgent reason, I'd suggest you discuss taking a beat, committing to wait an agreed upon amount of time to reflect before full withdrawing from all formal connection to their art. As we have covered previously, there are a lot of factors that go into interest, motivation, and consistency. Validate that you have heard your Creative and then suggest they sit on the decision for a bit, and ask if there is something they can do to change things up to see if that change helps them find interest in or passion for their art again.

It may be that they are in a not-so-fun part of their art. As the expectations and demands increase, what may have felt mostly fun and rewarding may have shifted into something that now feels more like work. If you as a parent feel there are compelling reasons for your Creative to continue in their art for at least a brief period longer, openly discuss those reasons with them. Make sure you are leaving time and space for your Creative to connect with what made them love their art in the first place. Discuss your expectations and any para-meters you may have for leaving that you want them to consider during this time.

Honor Commitments

Unless there is an emotional or physical crisis to be addressed, then, just like with any other activity, if this decision comes in the middle of a program, show, class, ensemble, team, or camp they have committed to, I would encourage you to tell your Creative that you expect them to honor their commitment—and offer to have a discussion regarding quitting after that time is up. Discuss the importance of follow-through, accountability, and giving their continued best effort to complete the activity. Using this time as a larger life lesson may be the most valuable part of this transition.

Perhaps you have a family expectation that all of your kids learn an instrument or participate in a physical activity such as dance through high school—an expectation that you have made clear to your Creative from the time they were young. Revisit that expectation with them and find out what might be done to honor this family commitment in some other way.

B was always pretty into photography. When he was in middle school, he really liked it, and our school district had a camp where he had a great experience every summer. He got a lot of attention for his composition and now, looking back, I think that was why, the summer after eighth grade, he was asking for all of this expensive gear. Up until then, it had still mostly been a hobby for him, so we held off. We told our kids they had to do at least one extracurricular at school, and B was our one kid who really had no idea what he wanted to do. He kind of fell into photography because that was what he knew.

So we eventually helped him get the gear he wanted, and he really became good. He spent a lot of time in his school's darkroom working on different developing techniques. But right after the beginning of his junior year, he was, I don't know, maybe kind of burned out, and he started to push [the idea of] quitting. We told him that he had to finish out the year since he had committed to being one of the yearbook photographers—and then the next year, he would have to replace it with something else. He knows we are pretty adamant that all of our high schoolers must be doing at least one school-sanctioned extracurricular, so he grumbled a lot, but he did it.

I don't know if he found something to connect with again or he just didn't want to find a new activity, but we noticed that, after mentioning quitting for a few months, he stopped talking about it and just kind of kept going. Senior year, he won a few awards for some of his photos, and that seemed to reignite his passion for a little bit. But before going to college, he told us he was going to sell some of his gear—which was hard to hear, but he'd honored his commitment and something had changed, so we gave him our blessing.

Ask Your Creative to Have a Plan

If your Creative's art has been a large part of their identity and social life and has been their primary activity, encourage them to have a plan to replace some of what the art gave them. A plan can help them look ahead to what it may feel like to no longer have their art filling the role it had in their life. Of course, what this looks like should connect with the reason they want to stop.

If they said they simply cannot give their art time and

energy with all of their other responsibilities, then the plan may be as simple as to not take on anything new for a bit while they see if their other responsibilities and activities truly do take up the new openings in their schedule. If it's a lack of interest, the plan may be for them to commit to exploring other activities—or even to explore other activities related to their art but in a new capacity.

If they say they need a break, then ask them to discuss this with the people involved and gain an understanding of what impact, if any, this may have on their ability to return to their art if and when they are ready. Commit to a timeframe to revisit the conversation and determine next steps following the break.

Allow Yourself and Your Teen Time to Transition

If, after all of this, your Creative is clear that they are ready to move on, it is important to allow both your Creative and yourself some time to grieve if you are experiencing the shift as a loss. Look for the positive lessons learned during your Creative's tenure in their art, celebrate the experience, and then, after processing the loss, look for ways to let it go. You may look up and discover your Creative has moved on to a new art they enjoy just as much or more and leaves them feeling more fulfilled.

Releasing an activity that has taken up so much time, so many resources, and so much energy can be a big change, both for your Creative and for you as a parent. For the Creative, if much of their identity was intertwined with their art, then they may feel a little lost. They may have hung on well past the point where they lost their love of their art out of fear or not knowing what else to do. To come to their parents and say "I want to move on" is hard and may leave them confused, anxious, or sad. Or the exact opposite may happen—they may feel total peace with the decision and be excited to move on to the next phase of exploration.

For you as a parent, if your Creative's art has been more than a general hobby, you may find it hard to move away from something that has played such a significant role in your relationship with them. If your Creative has worked for years on skill development and has achieved significant progress, it may be tempting to push them to keep going. It's important that you question your own motivations if you are tempted to actively discourage them from quitting, especially if they have a well-thought-out reason and a transition plan— even if you do not fully agree with their choice to transition.

Tell Them It's Okay To Move On

Once the decision has been made that your Creative is, in fact, moving on, offer them the gift of acceptance. Give them the message that you support this choice and that "quitting" after having put so much time, effort, and commitment into their art does not imply they are lazy, didn't follow through, or any other negative attribute. Talk about how interests change, how some things have a season and a reason, and offer them approval and support for any new ventures they would like to begin.

> I'm not gonna lie... I'd seen J show less and less interest in trumpet. He was so good, and it was such a joy to watch him. There was something about this little kid wailing away that just made me so proud. He used to play for hours—for fun. He was excited by every opportunity to play, and we worked to help him find them.
>
> One of these opportunities was an advanced jazz ensemble group on Sunday afternoons. It was over an hour drive from our house and lasted three hours, so I would just

stay. I became really tight with four other moms there, and we would go get coffee together and talk. But as J moved through middle school, he became less and less interested in his trumpet. The school orchestra was way below his level, and he preferred band music, but his friends were in orchestra, so he wanted to stay because that was the one period each day when he knew he'd be able to connect with them.

Finally, the summer before high school, J asked to quit his jazz ensemble and private lessons and only play in jazz band at his new high school. I'm not proud of this, but I told him no, absolutely not. He's spent too much time on it and had too much talent to just quit. So we told him he had to take lessons for one more year.

J's teacher called a few months later and said that J was clearly not really practicing. The teacher said that he typically only worked with college students and that maybe J should consider switching to a new teacher if he wasn't up for the rigor required. I was devastated. J was thrilled. That's when it hit me. I'd just done the thing I said I would never do: force my kid to do something they didn't like after they gave it a fair try. And I'm ashamed to admit that part of it, I realize now, was that I didn't want to give up the Sundays with my girlfriends. I loved driving J [to ensemble practice] —that was when we would catch up on the week, and [J would] usually talk way more than any other time. And I really enjoyed the time to connect with other women who were dealing with so many of the same things [my family was].

I had to take a good look at myself, and finally we let J quit. I could see he was just so much lighter. So far, he's barely touched his trumpet again. Instead, he walked in the door with a lacrosse stick a few months after quitting, and he was off in a new direction. And I'm learning to love cheering him on from the stands instead of from the audience and making friends with some of the other moms sitting there.

Change, both positive and negative, is inevitable and can be challenging to navigate. No matter what direction your Creative has chosen to move with their art, working to understand and support their decision to do so is one of the best ways to encourage developing autonomy and validate the lessons they have learned from their art.

Chapter 13

A Few Additional
Considerations

I have learned many lessons over time while raising three creatively driven kids. I am the first to admit that I make mistakes daily (sometimes hourly), and I'm still knee-deep in the experience. But on my best days, in my best moments, I am able to take the lessons I have learned over time and apply them in ways that I believe have helped my Creatives grow, learn, and flourish within their various arts. Only time will tell if they will continue to embrace their arts as major parts of their identities.

The oldest is already on his way. He is a young adult now and has chosen to make his art his career, and he is figuring out his path with increasing confidence. He knows we support his journey, whether it continues in the arts indefinitely or if, after some time, he wants to explore other ventures. But this current dive into his art has been a joy to watch, even when the road has had some inevitable bumps.

Our middle son is the one who has always seemed to be interested in little else. He seems to live in the world of creative arts, and it's hard for us to imagine that he won't continue in the creative world in some capacity. He is happily laying the foundations for this. Not always consistently—he still has moments where he gets distracted or discouraged or frustrated—but he also experiences great joy, satisfaction, and creative exploration within his arts of choice, and he is planning to merge these in some capacity down the line.

As for our youngest, it may be too early to say. He has plenty of time to change lanes, but as of now, creative art is a top priority. If the right situations and opportunities present themselves, he is actively preparing to take them and soar.

But as proud as I am of where my kids are today, some of the most important lessons I have learned have come from failures, missteps, missed opportunities, and misguided intentions. Over time, I've taken a step back and worked on being a better parent, using my clinical skills and parental instincts to be the most supportive and encouraging parent I can be to help our Creatives thrive in their arts.

Here are a few of the lessons I most often find myself coming back to.

ENCOURAGE EXPLORING OTHER INTERESTS

Depending on your Creative's interest level and dedication to a specific creative art, a natural narrowing down of activities may occur. If your tween dancer is making their way through a dance studio, there will be a natural increase in the core classes and styles they are required to focus on as they move upward. Perhaps faster than you may like, the many hours needed at the studio may leave very limited time—and budget—for any other activities outside of going to school, eating, sleeping, and taking some downtime with friends and family.

As your Creative gets older, this pruning of additional pursuits may become necessary, forcing the focus to become even more singular. This is especially true for high schoolers who may find themselves leaning into making their creative passion into their careers. If your budding videographer has the opportunity to explore filmmaking in their high school, it may be challenging for them not to take this class, thinking of how it will look on college applications or as practical life experience if they choose to forgo traditional college.

Yet they are still young, still learning, and still exploring. Support your teen or tween if they would like to use this time to explore some activities outside of their comfort zone. If they want to try a new sport, activity, or club, or a different art, sit down with them and help them figure out how to make it happen. If this means scaling back from their art for a bit, then let them know you value them trying new things and let them explore their new path.

In our family, only one of our kids has never really strayed from some form of art. Our other two have spent various amounts of time engaged in sports and other pursuits. Each time, they've always continued in their art of choice while doing so. When my oldest decided to stop basketball to prioritize guitar and musical theater, being in ensemble-based performance programs helped him fill the loss of being on a team sport. Ultimately, he found he preferred activities that included or complemented his art, and he lost any fear of missing out on other pursuits.

HELP TO SET REALISTIC GOALS

As a mom of two actors, I learned early on that praising effort and setting realistic goals is huge in establishing a healthy relationship to a creative art. In the world of actors, the job primarily consists of auditioning, not booking. Learning and understanding that is huge, and it changes how the actor looks at the process.

In our family, we celebrate callbacks. The further into the process our kids progress the more we celebrate—but we always celebrate each callback. We've also been known to offer up an unexpected small treat after particularly challenging auditions when our Creatives have put a lot of time and effort into preparation. We focus on growth, skill improvement, and honoring commitments. Of course, a booking is amazing, and for our kids, the ultimate reward for all of the hard work is being on set (or on the stage). But when their manager sends a "Wow, great job" text, we make sure to forward it and celebrate that *they are building their skills.*

LET THEM LEAD

Allowing your Creative to direct their own interest is one of the most important and challenging steps to engaging in a healthy parenting relationship. It's hard not to want to jump in and nudge (*ahem, shove*) them toward the skill they have shown an interest in and natural affinity for. It's hard to see them not properly prepare when you are spending hundreds or thousands of dollars on supporting their pursuit. It's hard to see them make questionable choices or decisions. But as a parent, to avoid stress, resentment, frustration, or a complete meltdown, stepping back and giving your Creative the majority of control is a necessary progression as they mature.

While in your Creative's younger years you likely gave them regimented schedules for practice and frequent reminders about assignments, projects, and other art-related responsibilities, once they move into their tween years, these should shift toward more open reminders: "Please remember to complete X before 7 p.m." As your Creative continues to mature, the goal should be to move to even less structured nudges—"Please practice today"—and eventually to only chiming in if you have reason to believe that practicing is not happening. I know all of my Creatives have gone through periods of not practicing unless asked. Sometimes it's because of boredom, sometimes it's to avoid a challenging goal, sometimes it's because they are just very busy, sometimes it's because they are distracted by their peers, and sometimes they simply aren't in the mood. As they've grown and come to better understand the impact of practice—especially the boring parts—on skill development, the cost of lessons and the overall sacrifice it takes for us as parents to both get them to lessons and pay for equipment, we loosen our hold on the reins and look to them to prepare. There have been some serious conversations about commitment at times, but in the end, they have regrouped and been grateful for it.

If you see your Creative struggling, you can—and I would argue *should*—offer supportive suggestions when you see an opening to do so. Also, know your Creative. My three boys are all very different. How much structure they need, how they work best, and what motivates them all impact when and how they practice. Over time, we've learned to tailor our approach to each of our sons' developmental stage and individual personality when deciding when and how to step in.

FOSTERING ACCOUNTABILITY AND GROWTH MINDSET

Remember to use a growth mindset when engaging with your Creative. When you're the person paying for the lessons, camps, seminars, equipment, workshops, supplies, studio time, membership fees, instrument repair, etc., it's hard not to become frustrated when your Creative is not giving their art their all. But encouraging them to both put their best effort in and appreciate that there will be moments of pain in the process without resorting to threats, manipulation, disappointment, and anger will be key for both your relationship with your Creative and your Creative's relationship with their art.

Focusing on a growth mindset in conversation means the feedback you give your Creative must come from a place of reinforcing room for, well, growth. Some examples of ways to engage with your Creative when they are feeling stuck, discouraged, frustrated, or disengaged with their progress include:

• "You're increasing your skills and that is the goal, even if it sometimes feels slow."

• "I hear you are frustrated. Why don't you stop now and allow yourself some time to refresh?"

• "You can always go back and work through mistakes once you get started."

• "Remember how far you've come. Think of where you started. You are making progress."

It also means working to avoid a negative cycle of begging, bribing, punishing, managing, or imposing deadlines on your Creative if they are not following through on skill building. This is their art, to love, to hate, to engage with, to ignore, and, ultimately, to develop in the way they want. Create a supportive, responsive environment and offer encouragement, but the older they are, the more you should back off. As they move into the latter teen years, they must have more accountability for taking ownership of their art.

THE FOUR AGREEMENTS

In his book *The Four Agreements*,[1] Don Miguel Ruiz offers a great framework that can be applied to your interactions with your Creative. Even if you aren't into the more "new age" packaging, the agreements themselves are advice that most people can relate to and implement in their lives.

The first agreement is "Be impeccable with your word." The idea here is that words are far more powerful than we realize, and they are the building blocks of concepts, beliefs, and labels. To avoid creating harmful situations, stop, think, and choose your words carefully. Creatives are often sensitive beings who take things to heart and may filter out the positive and focus on the negative or change their beliefs about their art based on too many thoughtless comments. *Be impeccable with your word.* Stop, think, and communicate in the most empathic, present, and safe manner that you can. I believe you will never regret taking this approach in any of your parenting interactions. Do your best to say what you mean with kindness, be clear in what you say, and, when in doubt, say nothing at all.

The second agreement is "Don't take anything personally." If you model and encourage this for your Creative, it will become an invaluable tool they can use to navigate tough situations. It is not a personal slight when your teen or tween doesn't win or place in a competition, does not get accepted into a program or school, or isn't cast in a role or chosen for an award. Do those things hurt? Yes. But if you can model focusing on the learning, the skill development, the experience, and the wisdom that come from those experiences, both you and your Creative will come away stronger.

The third agreement is "Don't make assumptions." With your Creative's art, do not make assumptions about what is going on in their head. Do not assume, based on your own personal interpretation of their actions, that they do not desire skill development, success, or mastery. Watch and listen, and do so without judgment. Ask open-ended, clarifying questions. Teach your Creative to do the same: do not assume the teacher has unrealistic expectations, ask questions. Why do they want you to do something a certain way?

With one of my sons, I began to question his desire to pursue a specific skill he claimed he wanted to learn. Even though he had all the pieces available to him, he only seemed to be making limited progress and putting in limited time. At one point, I was convinced the disconnect between his words and actions suggested he didn't truly have an investment in learning this new skill.

Instead of acting on this assumption, I took a step back, and I came to realize that part of the issue was he really did not like working on this skill in isolation. The shared equipment he needed was kept in a location away from the main action of the house. For me, when I was learning something new or engaging in work that required concentration, it was great. But for him, it wasn't; until he had better mastery and could become fully engrossed in a productive way, he didn't enjoy the isolation from the rest of the household. I began bringing my work to the room he was working in, and, suddenly, he began to make far more sustained progress.

Let me be clear: I know nothing about the skill he was learning. I was not guiding him or helping him; I was, in fact, on my laptop with headphones on, doing my own work. Yet just my presence helped. And, ultimately, we eventually gifted him his own equipment (as opposed to the shared equipment in our home office), which allowed him to work in his room on the second floor of our home, where there is usually someone around if he wants connection, or to close his door when he prefers focused concentration.

Had I continued down the path of assuming he was not

very serious about this new skill, my interactions with him around his art could have been discouraging and damaging and may have potentially shut down his skill development. By sitting back and observing and trying to understand why his actions might not be in line with his words, I was able to develop a new approach for how to best support him.

Don't make assumptions about your Creative's progress or lack thereof. Watch, ask open questions, offer opportunities for a new approach, and see what truth your teen or tween offers you.

The final agreement is "Always do your best." Doing your best is the recognition that we, as humans, have good and bad days and good and bad moments. The goal should be to always do your best in the present moment. Just as the best parenting you could manage today may not be the best you could offer yesterday, the best output your Creative can manage today might not always be quite as good as the best they could do yesterday, but that does not mean they aren't still doing their best. Encourage them to understand and embrace these fluctuations in their work. As long as they can honestly, truly say that they are doing the best they can in any given moment, they—and you— cannot ask or expect more of themselves. Focus on and celebrate the effort, not the outcome. There will be many moments in life where the outcome may not be what your Creative had hoped, or even what they'd been capable of days earlier, and, at those times, they may feel frustrated that they are not making progress. If they are able to give themselves grace because they know they did the best they could, they may avoid frustration or discouragement and know that, the next time that they try, the outcome may be more in alignment with the desired outcome. This can be a hard practice to learn, so try to model it for your Creative.

I remember once, my son had a very large musical theater

audition with a large singing part. He prepared, we got him vocal coaching, and he had presented a very consistent, outstanding performance for the entire week before the audition. He walked in with confidence, but he came back out uncertain. When we got to the car, I asked him how he felt, and he said he felt that his acting was great and he'd done well vocally, but even though he'd warmed up properly and he wasn't feeling nervous, his voice just wasn't at its best. He expressed some frustration that, up until it "counted," he'd nailed the vocals. We talked about the fact that he'd done all he could, that he had walked in and done his absolute best right at that moment, and as long as he could honestly say that was his truth, then he had to be satisfied with that and let it go.

We drove home, and he went to his room, saying he was tired—a normal post-audition wind-down for him. A few hours later, he came downstairs and said, "Mom, I'm pretty sure I'm getting sick. I fell asleep and I woke up freezing cold and now I'm getting congested and sneezing."

Sure enough, he was spiking a fever, which turned into a horrible, down-for-the-count-for-three-days type of virus. He truly *had* done his best in the audition. We had no way of knowing he was getting sick. If the symptoms had hit a few hours earlier, we would have requested to try to reschedule. But that is not how it happened, and that is life.

Support and praise your teen or tween for meeting each moment with the best they can give, and move on. Life is ever-changing; their best in the next moment may look different. There will always be good days and bad days, good moments and bad moments. Just remind your Creative to always do their best.

RELUCTANCE TO BE IN THE SPOTLIGHT

Many parents remember a time when their Creative was younger and openly and happily shared their art. They brought you their latest drawing with joy and beamed with pride as you hung it prominently on your refrigerator. They turned the karaoke machine as loud as it could go and belted out their favorite songs. They happily moved the coffee table out of the way and turned the family room into a dance studio where they would spend hours creating choreography from an unlimited imagination. There was a freedom and purity in their enjoyment, and having an audience typically only added to their experience.

This open sharing of your Creative's art may diminish as they approach the teen or tween years. As they move into this developmental stage, the social pressure to conform, fit in, and not stand out increases. Conforming to expectations and avoiding drawing attention to themselves is part of the beginning stages of their developmental need to separate from you (the parent) and find their own identity.

In the beginning, this can look like the exact opposite of developing their own identity. In many cases, it looks like mass imitation. If you've ever been in a public middle school, you may notice that even without the limitation of a school uniform, what you tend to see are variations of the same few looks. While when your Creative begs to dye their hair purple it may feel radical and very much like an effort to be as different as possible from both you and others, upon crossing the threshold of the school, you may find dyed hair is a common theme. The important thing is that their new look differentiates them from you or your family, the people they have most identified with up until now.

As your Creative gets older, you may notice two things: a diminishing of open creativity and an unwillingness to share their art. Sharing goes from being a rewarding and open process to being a risky one, one they may avoid in order to steer clear of any unwanted attention and keep from being seen as "showing off."

As a society, we receive very mixed messages about "shining." One minute, we are being told, "Go, do your thing—be great! If someone can't handle it, that is their problem." In the next, we may be told, "Be humble," with the implication that those who are not humble are bragging or boastful. We are encouraged to undervalue our successes and appear modest or downplay our skills. For teens or tweens, the safer part of this messaging often falls firmly on the side of avoiding sharing the extent of their skills or not sharing those skills at all.

For parents, this can be a frustrating experience—just as your Creative's hard work and skill development is really paying off, they may pull back. To show up and put their best art in the spotlight can be a vulnerable task, even in the most accepting of environments. By asking them to do so in a place where standing out may be seen as an ego-driven desire may invite pushback and even rejection by peers. Try to remember that, even if your Creative finds the courage to step onto the proverbial (or literal) stage, they have to step back off and into the culture of their peers, who may respond with little or no enthusiasm—or worse, with negative feedback or alienation.

This is hard for anyone, but for someone who is trying to find their own identity and is still learning resilience, it may be simply too much of a hurdle. They may simply refuse to "shine" in a public forum, no matter how much you or their instructors, teachers, and coaches encourage them to share their art. Give them the space to pull back. Watch and see where, if anywhere, they are willing to risk a little more and share their passion. Their reluctance does not mean they are not invested in their art or they do not care about it.

One of my clients brought that exact concern to me. She indicated that she and her daughter were butting heads about her daughter's refusal to perform in public. Her daughter had a beautiful voice, had been working on her craft for years, and had performed publicly many times in the past. But sometime in middle school, she began to refuse to perform anywhere other than in her school musicals. Her mother was baffled as her daughter was willing to perform at school—often as the lead—but stopped participating in all other opportunities. My client was fine with her daughter's tentative plan to become a professional performer, but my client felt that, in order for her daughter to further develop her stage presence and performance skills, she needed to be actively seeking opportunities to perform whenever she could. My client's job involved speaking to large audiences, and she understood the value of experience with "working the room."

After speaking with the mom, I asked her to go back to her daughter with some open-ended questions to try to engage in a more productive dialogue with her. Eventually, her daughter felt safe enough to share her experiences with her mom. The daughter told her that another student at her school had seen her perform at an event in another town and had characterized her as an attention-seeker. This girl told their peers that my client's daughter felt she was "too good" for just the school musical and she "thinks she's famous or something."

My client was stunned to hear this, as she knew exactly when this had occurred since the other girl and her mother had come up to her and inquired about how her daughter had obtained the opportunity. My client had been confused because this school had a strong arts program and there was no social stigma associated with being in the school musicals, so she didn't understand why anyone wouldn't support a performer doing something outside of that context. My client understood this reaction as jealousy and wanted to talk her daughter out of caring what her "insecure peers" thought. She felt this would be necessary to "survive" in the world of entertainment.

I walked my client through the impracticality of this desire for her daughter at this moment in life and the complexity of all the factors at play. Yes, jealousy was a likely culprit, but understanding where her daughter was developmentally was important as well. She was new to the school, she was finding her place, and she wanted to fly below the radar for a bit before she made any decisions about sharing her skills. My client ultimately pulled back and let her daughter choose when and where to perform, and by the time her daughter was in high school, she had a strong friend group that gave her a sense of social support and validation that allowed her to engage in more large community performances without concern for what those outside of her friend group thought.

MENTAL TOUGHNESS VERSUS EMOTIONAL CONNECTION

The client above had a very successful career that did not fall under the umbrella of the creative arts. As a woman in a male-dominated field, she'd learned mental toughness in order to survive being passed over unfairly or being held to a different standard than her male peers. She'd learned that the more opportunities she took that forced her to disconnect from her emotions and take command of a room or stage, the more comfortable and powerful her presentations became.

Her experiences and eventual success in her field had led

her to want to impart the importance of mental toughness to her daughters from a young age. With her older daughter, her definition of mental toughness had worked well; that daughter was a soccer player who had benefited from learning early on to not let things get to her. My client had advised and encouraged her oldest daughter to compartmentalize and ignore her physical and emotional pain when she was on the field, a strategy that benefited her. Her performance did increase when she learned to "ignore" her emotional state and focus on the task at hand.

This did not work for my client's Creative. She realized how different her two daughters were when, at a young age, her singer told her, "I always sing better when I'm a little sad." Her connection with and ability to embrace of her emotional states was essential to her emotional presence when performing.

I've seen performers—and, sadly, occasionally coaches and instructors in the creative world—confuse the idea of being "mentally tough" with being out of touch with one's emotional state. These two things are not necessarily the same, and one can be mentally tough while still being connected to their internal emotional world. Being mentally tough is a constellation of skills and does not require disconnecting from emotional states but rather learning how to use and manage those emotional states in a constructive manner.

Mental toughness includes emotional resilience, motivation, focus, self-belief, knowing your why, and having the ability to perform under pressure. It develops stronger artists, and one can be mentally tough while still being emotionally connected and vulnerable and sharing openly.

Teach your Creative that their emotions can be used to enhance their art. Surround them with teachers and mentors who understand this and who teach identifying and honoring emotions, work with your Creative to minimize self-judgment around their emotional state, and create safe environments in which your Creative can explore and harness their emotions constructively in their art.

SOME ADULTS WILL TEAR TEENS AND TWEENS DOWN

This may sound crazy, but I've met many parents of Creatives —and many Creatives themselves—with stories about adults who had no problem sharing openly critical, non-constructive, demeaning, and often mean-spirited remarks about teen or tween artists. I've witnessed adults criticizing a musical theater performance within earshot of the teen or tween who'd just performed. I've seen an art instructor tear apart a winning painting at a high school competition without knowing if the artist was in the room (he was). I've personally experienced a parent coming up to me after my son's band had just won a contest for the second year in a row to offer her opinion that the completely different panel of judges was unfairly biased toward my son's band as opposed to her son's band. I've heard countless stories of variations of this theme, and it's disheartening.

As painful as this might be for your Creative to hear from some adult they have no connection to, it's much more damaging when it comes from someone who they consider as an authority figure—a parent of another Creative, an instructor, a well-respected coach.

When a Creative is confronted with malicious and hurtful comments from an adult, they often do not know how to respond in the moment. Good, obedient teens and tweens have been taught to respect adults and not talk back. They rarely challenge people who are in positions of authority. And outside of the very obvious problems with adults who feel free to communicate with teens or tweens in this manner, there are also some larger issues that can manifest from these types of interactions.

Teens and tweens can be very easily influenced by their environment. If that environment contains negative, limiting voices in positions of authority, Creatives can very quickly begin to believe in the negative feedback. They may begin to embrace limiting beliefs about their abilities. For this reason, it is very important to encourage your teen or tween to be a critical thinker regarding a person's motivation to make negative comments. Of course, this begins long before the teen or tween years, but it is essential for protecting your Creative's mindset against those who do not believe in big dreams, those who don't appreciate the skill and vulnerability it takes to put yourself out there, and those who handle disappointment with jealousy and by tearing down others rather than by building themselves or others up in community.

If you as a parent are concerned about how your child's mentor, coach, instructor, or teacher is communicating with your teen or tween, do not ignore your concern. Talk to your Creative, and closely watch what happens during their interactions. Do not be afraid to shift gears if the fit is wrong or potentially damaging. The right instructor for your Creative will push them to excellence without causing emotional pain.

NO COMPARISON ALLOWED

It's been said that "Comparison is the thief of joy." I cannot think of a more appropriate phrase to rinse and repeat often with your Creative.

It's human nature to look around and see what others are doing. We are naturally social beings—and we can learn a lot from watching what is going on around us. But watching and learning is not the same as watching and comparing. Unfortunately, many programs in the arts may be set up to inadvertently create an undercurrent of comparison. Auditions, competitions, class placement, public performances, and exhibitions—even something as simple as putting every student's art up on the wall to celebrate—can lead to unhealthy patterns of comparison if we, as parents, have not worked to inoculate our Creatives against this pointless endeavor.

Creativity needs individuality. It needs the unique spin and point of view your Creative can bring to a painting, choreography, composition, performance, video, or photograph. Remind your Creative of what made them fall in love with their art in the first place. The fun, the freedom, the ability to, well, *create* from nothing. If you see them falling into a negative headspace of looking at others as a measure of their progress or success, suggest they work on focusing on little things about their own journey that they are proud of. The benchmark should never be someone else's accomplishments, but rather who we are as individuals and how we have made progress.

This reminder is one we adults may need as well. You must also refrain from the temptation to compare, both in your own life and in your Creative's. Put on your blinders, practice gratitude, and focus on your Creative's incremental skill building. Every journey is unique—if they love their art, they will find their own way, and it will be amazing.

Chapter 14

Conclusion

Creative minds have their own set of wants, needs, and desires around their art of choice. They often describe themselves as experiencing the world in a unique way, which leads to unique ways of navigating their inner and outer worlds. Creative teens and tweens are some of my favorite humans to engage with. I love their unique perspective, enthusiasm, excitement, wonderment, and questioning, and how they don't accept the status quo as the approach they must take. I'm often in awe of their ability to cause me to think about things in new ways.

This book was never written with the intention of creating a comprehensive guide to raising teens or tweens drawn to the creative arts. Instead, it is the book I wish someone had handed me when my kids were younger and I was trying my best to piece together various sources of information so I could be as present and supportive as possible in their creative pursuits. My hope is that the information in this book provides you with some additional insight into how to better relate to, support, and guide your teen or tween Creative in connection to their art.

You are the best expert on your teen or tween. You know which of the concepts discussed throughout this book resonate with you and your experiences with your teen or tween and which don't fit. I know for me, although my boys' deep interest in and love for various arts is a commonality they share, parenting each one has been very different.

One of my sons has always been motivated to practice. I rarely needed to tune in to how much he was preparing; he managed to get it done. The few times when not preparing enough caused him to not meet goals he'd hoped to reach, that consequence led him to prepare more going forward. At this point, any time he may be inclined to avoid or postpone practice, he knows what he needs to do to get things done. When he is met with mental blocks, he seeks ways to work through them—occasionally with our input, but lately, most often on his own. He's actively applying the lessons his art has taught him about perseverance and resilience.

One of my sons is more inclined to work on the things he has mastered and is very skilled at, but he sometimes struggles to put the work in on the skills that are necessary but boring. He's getting there. He may say, "It's so *booooorrrrrrrii-iiinnnnnnggg...*" but I will also hear him working on those skills in his own way. I have no doubt that he will find his unique path to getting things done. Over time, he's come to understand how much he enjoys working in groups and collaborative settings. He is, however, also inclined to do a solo deep dive once he gets himself going—and when that magic hits, he will spend hours working on something until he gets it right.

And one of my sons still needs occasional reminders, some of which are met with no resistance and others with a sigh and promises to get to it later. Knowing he is my Questioner, I come prepared with an explanation of why certain things are potentially boring or frustrating but to his benefit. He's becoming better at time-management, getting things done when he knows there is something he'd like to do later on without interruption. He is also the one who may or may not continue his journey in the arts. For now, he says he is 100 percent committed, but he's young enough that we are continuing to support his exploration of other interests as well—though we truly won't be shocked if he continues down a path where some type of creativity is a central theme in his future.

Life has a way of making unexpected turns. I am having the absolute best time with my artistic kids. Though I'm happy to attend and support whatever activities they want to focus on, I'm also pretty happy with a life filled with live music, performances, and the arts in general. Of course, these most often represent the happy moments, when the hard work has been completed, the skills have come together, and there is a moment to shine and reap the rewards of making it through the challenging moments. I fully acknowledge that there are plenty of tough times too, times when, try as they might, my Creatives struggle with new skills, when they have less-than-great performances, when they aren't so sure they want to keep going. But I also know that this would be true of any other endeavors they chose; it's part of life and learning.

If you are reading this book and made it this far, it's more than clear that you are deeply committed to being the best parent you can be to the Creative teen or tween you have been gifted with. I think this is true of most parents in general. We want to see our children be happy and thrive and move into adulthood as well-balanced, financially independent, fulfilled, kind, generous, loving humans. We're all out here just doing the best we can in each moment.

After you close this book, I would like to ask you to take a minute to process just how far your Creative has already come in their art. Pull up one of their early paintings on your phone. Find a video of them singing in preschool. Look at the framed photo they took that first told you they could see something special from behind the lens. Look at the program from their first recital or the playbill from their first play. It is the dedication, love, and skills you have already brought to your Creative as their parent that have led to the skill level they have today.

The world needs the arts. Thank you for sharing and nurturing your Creative's interest in the arts and helping them to bring a little more joy, understanding, empathy, excitement, and relatability to the larger world. I can't wait to see all the amazing art they release into this world and how far they soar with your dedication to parenting talent.

Further Reading

Daring Greatly: How the Courage to Be Vulnerable Transforms the Way We Live, Love, Parent and Lead by Brené Brown

The Gifts of Imperfection by Brené Brown

Mindset: The New Psychology of Success by Carol Dweck

The Big Leap: Conquer Your Hidden Fear and Take Life to the Next Level by Gay Hendricks

The Teenage Brain: A Neuroscientist's Survival Guide to Raising Adolescents and Young Adults by Frances E. Jensen with Amy Ellis Nutt

The Four Tendencies: The Indispensable Personality Profiles That Reveal How to Make Your Life Better (and Other People's Lives Better, Too) by Gretchen Rubin

Acknowledgments

To my husband, Kermit, who is the best partner not only in parenting three creative, artistic, kind young men, but in all of life. Thank you for always having my back and being my biggest supporter in anything I do. Thank you for being an incredible role model of integrity, work ethic, and loving support and encouragement for our boys. All these years and you are still my best friend. I'm not exactly sure how I manifested you, but I am deeply grateful that I did. Live/love you.

To my three amazing sons, Alex, Zach, and Gabe. Raising you is the honor and privilege of my life. Your desire to explore creative realms has inspired me to learn more, work to support you better, and up my game as a human. I hope you will forgive me the (many) mistakes I've made as well as the ones I will inevitably make in the future. Always know that no one watching you learn and accomplish your goals, both small and large, is more excited, proud, and impressed by you than Dad and I. The fact that you are all compassionate, generous, thoughtful humans makes me feel like somehow, some way, we are doing something right.

To Ingrid, who has been there longer than either of us wants to calculate. From dating, to weddings, to marriage and stories from the parenting trenches, knowing you are in my corner with unwavering support, laughter, and (when needed) some wine is a gift. Thank you for being you.

Allison—from the moment I said I had a full book outline, you didn't just say "go for it," you led by example with guidance and generosity. You have been the most supportive example of an abundance mindset in action.

To all of Girlpower, the best model of what female friendships should be: honesty, emotional support, mutual respect, and lots of laughter. Framily forever.

Darci—I could not have asked for a better person to help lead the charge for the boys' goals and dreams. I am so grateful to have you in our corner—and to call you my friend.

To my editor, Yna Davis. From our first meeting, I knew you were the right person to usher me to the finish line. Thank you for making the last phase of book writing truly a pleasure.

A sincere and huge thank you to the parents of creative tweens, teens, and young adults who so generously took time out of their busy schedules to fill out my detailed questionnaire and answer follow-up questions or to allow me to interview you. The way you shared your personal stories, words of wisdom, honest vulnerability, and good and bad moments as you too tried to figure out how to best do this helps us all. If no one has told you lately, you are amazing, simply because you are there and you care so deeply for your kids. Thank you for sharing a small part of your journey with me. Your kids are so very lucky to have you.

Lastly, thank you to all the truly amazing teachers, coaches, workshop leaders, agents, managers, directors, friends, childcare providers, and fellow parents of Creatives who have shaped, supported, guided, cared about, and showed up for our boys along the way. It takes a village and wow, did my boys manifest an amazing one.

NOTES

THE "TALENT" TRAP

1. Oxford Languages, s.v. "talent (n.)," accessed December 22, 2022, https://www.google.com/search?q=definition+of+talent.
2. Julian B. Rotter, "Generalized Expectancies for Internal Versus External Control of Reinforcement," *Psychological Monographs: General and Applied* 80, no. 1 (1966): 1–28. https://doi.org/10.1037/h0092976.

MOTIVATION FOR CREATION

1. Anthony F. Gregorc, *An Adult's Guide to Style* (Columbia, CT: Gregorc Associates, 1982), 74.
2. Gregorc, *An Adult's Guide to Style*, 74.
3. Gretchen Rubin, *Better Than Before: Mastering the Habits of Our Everyday Lives* (New York: Crown, 2015).
4. Gretchen Rubin, *The Four Tendencies: The Indispensable Personality Profiles That Reveal How to Make Your Life Better (and Other People's Lives Better, Too)* (New York: Harmony Books, 2017), 272.

PERFECTIONISM AND PROCRASTINATION

1. Brené Brown, *The Gifts of Imperfection* (Minneapolis, MN: Hazelden Information & Educational Services, 2010).
2. Alice Lo and Maree J. Abbott, "Review of the Theoretical, Empirical, and Clinical Status of Adaptive and Maladaptive Perfectionism," *Behaviour Change* 30, no. 2 (2013): 96–116.

MINDSET, FEAR, AND ANXIETY

1. Carol S. Dweck, *Mindset: The New Psychology of Success* (New York: Ballantine Books, 2007), 320.
2. Martin M. Broadwell, "Teaching for Learning (XVI.)," *The Gospel Guardian* 20, no. 41 (1969): 1–3a.
3. Linda Adams, "Learning a New Skill Is Easier Said than Done," Gordon Training International, accessed December 22, 2022, https://www.

gordontraining.com/free-workplace-articles/learning-a-new-skill-is-easier-said-than-done/.

4. Chris Drew, "5 Stages of Learning (Levels of Learning Ladder)," Helpful-Professor.com, last revised November 1, 2022, https://helpfulprofessor.com/stages-of-learning/.

5. Frances E. Jensen, *The Teenage Brain: A Neuroscientist's Survival Guide to Raising Adolescents and Young Adults* (New York: Harper Paperbacks, 2016), 384.

6. Katharine B. Parodi et al. "Time Trends and Disparities in Anxiety among Adolescents, 2012–2018," *Social Psychiatry and Psychiatric Epidemiology* 57, no. 1 (2022): 127–137, https://doi.org/10.1007/s00127-021-02122-9.

7. Nicholas B. Allen, "Cognitive Therapy of Depression. Aaron T Beck, A John Rush, Brian F Shaw, Gary Emery. New York: Guilford Press, 1979," *The Australian and New Zealand Journal of Psychiatry* 36, no. 2 (2002): 275–278, https://doi.org/10.1046/j.1440-1614.2002.t01-5-01015.x.

8. Fred Luskin and Ken Pelletier, *Stress Free for Good: 10 Scientifically Proven Life Skills for Health and Happiness* (San Francisco: HarperOne Publishers, 2005), 223.

FAILURE, LIMITING BELIEFS, AND ACCOUNTABILITY

1. Kyla Haimovitz and Carol S. Dweck, "What Predicts Children's Fixed and Growth Intelligence Mind-Sets? Not Their Parents' Views of Intelligence but Their Parents' Views of Failure," *Psychological Science* 27, no. 6 (2016): 859–869, https://doi.org/10.1177/0956797616639727.

2. Megan McArdle, *The Up Side of Down: Why Failing Well Is the Key to Success* (New York: Penguin Books, 2015), 320.

3. Gay Hendricks, *The Big Leap: Conquer Your Hidden Fear and Take Life to the Next Level* (San Francisco: HarperOne Publishers, 2010), 224.

NEGATIVITY BIAS, VULNERABILITY, SHAME, AND RESILIENCE

1. Tiffany A. Ito, John T. Cacioppo, and Peter J. Lang, "Eliciting Affect Using the International Affective Picture System: Trajectories through Evaluative Space," *Personality and Social Psychology Bulletin* 24, no. 8 (1998): 855–879, https://doi.org/10.1177/01461672982480.

2. Tiffany A. Ito et al. "Negative Information Weighs More Heavily on the Brain: The Negativity Bias in Evaluative Categorizations," *Journal of Personality and Social Psychology* 75, no. 4 (1998): 887–900, https://doi.org/10.1037/0022-3514.75.4.887.

3. Roy F. Baumeister et al. "Bad Is Stronger than Good," *Review of General Psychology* 5, no. 4 (2001): 323–370, https://doi.org/10.1037/1089-2680.5.4.323.
4. Brené Brown, *Daring Greatly: How the Courage to Be Vulnerable Transforms the Way We Live, Love, Parent, and Lead* (New York: Avery, 2015), 34.
5. Brown, *Daring Greatly, 34.*
6. Brown, *Daring Greatly, 320.*
7. "Warning Signs of Mental Illness," American Psychiatric Association, accessed December 3, 2022, https://www.psychiatry.org/patients-families/warning-signs-of-mental-illness.

MENTAL HEALTH CONCERNS

1. "Warning Signs of Mental Illness."

OTHER CONSIDERATIONS

1. "Student Reports of Bullying: Results from the 2017 School Crime Supplement to the National Crime Victimization Survey," National Center for Education Statistics, July 2019, https://nces.ed.gov/pubs2019/2019054.pdf [PDF].
2. "Preventing Bullying," Centers for Disease Control and Prevention, 2019, https://www.cdc.gov/violenceprevention/pdf/yv/bullying-fact sheet508.pdf [PDF].
3. Gianluca Gini and Tiziana Pozzoli, "Bullied Children and Psychosomatic Problems: A Meta-Analysis," *Pediatrics* 132, no. 4 (2013): 720–729, https://doi.org/10.1542/peds.2013-0614.
4. Gini and Pozzoli, "Bullied Children and Psychosomatic Problems."
5. Sherri Gordon, "10 Types of Kids Most Likely to Be Bullied," Verywell Family, last updated March 25, 2021, https://www.verywellfamily.com/reasons-why-kids-are-bullied-460777.

EMOTIONAL AND PHYSICAL SAFETY ON SOCIAL MEDIA

1. Emily A. Vogels, Risa Gelles-Watnick, and Navid Massarat, "Teens, Social Media and Technology 2022," Pew Research Center, August 10, 2022, https://www.pewresearch.org/internet/2022/08/10/teens-social-media-and-technology-2022/.
2. Victoria Rideout et al. "The Common Sense Census: Media Use by Tweens and Teens, 2021," Common Sense Media, March 9, 2022,

https://www.commonsensemedia.org/research/the-common-sense-census-media-use-by-tweens-and-teens-2021.

3. Megan McCluskey, "How Addictive Social Media Algorithms Could Finally Face a Reckoning in 2022," E&P, January 4, 2022, https://www.editorandpublisher.com/stories/how-addictive-social-media-algorithms-could-finally-face-a-reckoning-in-2022,214063.

4. Lucas Galan et al. "How Young People Consume News and the Implications for Mainstream Media," Reuters Institute for the Study of Journalism, 2019, https://reutersinstitute.politics.ox.ac.uk/our-research/how-young-people-consume-news-and-implications-mainstream-media.

"New Survey Reveals Teens Get Their News from Social Media and YouTube," Common Sense Media, August 12, 2019, https://www.commonsensemedia.org/press-releases/new-survey-reveals-teens-get-their-news-from-social-media-and-youtube.

BEING THE PARENT YOUR CREATIVE NEEDS

1. Teresa Wiseman, "Concept Analysis of Empathy," *Journal of Advanced Nursing* 23, no. 6 (1996):1162–1167, https://doi.org/10.1046/j.1365-2648.1996.12213.x.

A FEW ADDITIONAL CONSIDERATIONS

1. Don Miguel Ruiz, *The Four Agreements: A Practical Guide to Personal Freedom* (San Rafael, CA: Amber-Allen Publishing, 2001).

Bibliography

Adams, Linda Adams. "Learning a New Skill Is Easier Said than Done." Gordon Training International. Accessed December 22, 2022. https://www.gordontraining.com/free-workplace-articles/learning-a-new-skill-is-easier-said-than-done/.

Allen, Nicholas B. "Cognitive Therapy of Depression. Aaron T Beck, A John Rush, Brian F Shaw, Gary Emery. New York: Guilford Press, 1979." *The Australian and New Zealand Journal of Psychiatry* 36, no. 2 (2002): 275–278. https://doi.org/10.1046/j.1440-1614.2002.t01-5-01015.x.

Baumeister, Roy F., Ellen Bratslavsky, Catrin Finkenauer, and Kathleen D. Vohs. "Bad Is Stronger than Good." *Review of General Psychology* 5, no. 4 (2001): 323–370. https://doi.org/10.1037/1089-2680.5.4.323.

Broadwell, Martin M. "Teaching for Learning (XVI.)." *The Gospel Guardian* 20, no. 41 (1969): 1–3a.

Brown, Brené. *The Gifts of Imperfection*. Minneapolis, MN: Hazelden Information & Educational Services, 2010.

Brown, Brené. *Daring Greatly: How the Courage to Be Vulnerable Transforms the Way We Live, Love, Parent, and Lead*. New York: Avery, 2015.

Drew, Chris. "5 Stages of Learning (Levels of Learning Ladder)." HelpfulProfessor.com. Last revised November 1, 2022. https://helpfulprofessor.com/stages-of-learning/.

Dweck, Carol S. *Mindset: The New Psychology of Success*. New York: Ballantine Books, 2007.

Galan, Lucas, Jordan Osserman, Tim Parker, and Matt Taylor. "How Young People Consume News and the Implications for Mainstream Media."

Reuters Institute for the Study of Journalism, 2019. https://reutersinsti tute.politics.ox.ac.uk/our-research/how-young-people-consume-news-and-implications-mainstream-media.

Gini, Gianluca, and Tiziana Pozzoli. "Bullied Children and Psychosomatic Problems: A Meta-Analysis." *Pediatrics* 132, no. 4 (2013): 720–729. https://doi.org/10.1542/peds.2013-0614.

Gordon, Sherri. "10 Types of Kids Most Likely to Be Bullied." Verywell Family. Last updated March 25, 2021. https://www.verywellfamily.com/reasons-why-kids-are-bullied-460777.

Gregorc, Anthony F. *An Adult's Guide to Style.* Columbia, CT: Gregorc Associates, 1982.

Haimovitz, Kyla, and Carol S. Dweck. "What Predicts Children's Fixed and Growth Intelligence Mind-Sets? Not Their Parents' Views of Intelligence but Their Parents' Views of Failure." *Psychological Science* 27, no. 6 (2016): 859–869. https://doi.org/10.1177/0956797616639727.

Hendricks, Gay. *The Big Leap: Conquer Your Hidden Fear and Take Life to the Next Level.* San Francisco: HarperOne Publishers, 2010.

Ito, Tiffany A., John T. Cacioppo, and Peter J. Lang. "Eliciting Affect Using the International Affective Picture System: Trajectories through Evaluative Space." *Personality and Social Psychology Bulletin* 24, no. 8 (1998): 855–879. https://doi.org/10.1177/01461672982480.

Ito, Tiffany A., J.T. Larsen, N.K. Smith, and John T. Cacioppo. "Negative Information Weighs More Heavily on the Brain: The Negativity Bias in Evaluative Categorizations." *Journal of Personality and Social Psychology* 75, no. 4 (1998): 887–900. https://doi.org/10.1037/0022-3514.75.4.887.

Jensen, Frances E. *The Teenage Brain: A Neuroscientist's Survival Guide to Raising Adolescents and Young Adults.* New York: Harper Paperbacks, 2016.

Lo, Alice, and Maree J. Abbott. "Review of the Theoretical, Empirical, and Clinical Status of Adaptive and Maladaptive Perfectionism." *Behaviour Change* 30, no. 2 (2013): 96–116.

Luskin, Fred, and Ken Pelletier. *Stress Free for Good: 10 Scientifically Proven Life Skills for Health and Happiness.* San Francisco: HarperOne Publishers, 2005.

McArdle, Megan. *The Up Side of Down: Why Failing Well Is the Key to Success.* New York: Penguin Books, 2015.

McCluskey, Megan. "How Addictive Social Media Algorithms Could Finally Face a Reckoning in 2022." E&P, January 4, 2022. https://www.editorand publisher.com/stories/how-addictive-social-media-algorithms-could-finally-face-a-reckoning-in-2022,214063.

Morgan, Rachel E., and Alexandra Thompson. "The National Crime Victimization Survey: School Crime Supplement." Online survey, Bureau of Justice Statistics, 1989–2019. https://bjs.ojp.gov/data-collection/school-crime-supplement-scs.

"New Survey Reveals Teens Get Their News from Social Media and YouTube."

Common Sense Media, August 12, 2019. https://www.commonsenseme dia.org/press-releases/new-survey-reveals-teens-get-their-news-from-social-media-and-youtube.

Oxford Languages, s.v. "talent (n.)." Accessed December 22, 2022. https://www.google.com/search?q=definition+of+talent.

Parodi, Katharine B., Melissa K. Holt, Jennifer Greif Green, Michelle V. Porche, Brian Koenig, and Ziming Xuan. "Time Trends and Disparities in Anxiety Among Adolescents, 2012–2018." *Social Psychiatry and Psychiatric Epidemiology* 57, no. 1 (2022): 127–137. https://doi.org/10.1007/s00127-021-02122-9.

Patchin, Justin W., and Sameer Hinduja. "Tween Cyberbullying in 2020." Cyberbullying Research Center, September 30, 2020. https://i.cartoonnet work.com/stop-bullying/pdfs/CN_Stop_Bullying_Cyber_Bullying_Re port_9.30.20.pdf [PDF].

Perren, Sonja, Idean Ettekal, and Gary Ladd. "The Impact of Peer Victimiza-tion on Later Maladjustment: Mediating and Moderating Effects of Hostile and Self-Blaming Attributions." *Journal of Child Psychology and Psychiatry* 54, no. 1 (2013): 46–55. https://doi.org/10.1111/j.1469-7610.2012.02618.x.

"Preventing Bullying." Centers for Disease Control and Prevention, 2019. https://www.cdc.gov/violenceprevention/pdf/yv/bullying-fact sheet508.pdf [PDF].

Rideout, Victoria, Alanna Peebles, Supreet Mann, and Michael B. Robb. "The Common Sense Census: Media Use by Tweens and Teens, 2021." Common Sense Media, March 9, 2022. https://www.commonsensemedi-a.org/research/the-common-sense-census-media-use-by-tweens-and-teens-2021.

Rotter, Julian B. "Generalized Expectancies for Internal Versus External Control of Reinforcement." *Psychological Monographs: General and Applied* 80, no. 1 (1966): 1–28. https://doi.org/10.1037/h0092976.

Rubin, Gretchen. *Better Than Before: Mastering the Habits of Our Everyday Lives.* New York: Crown, 2015.

Ruiz, Don Miguel. *The Four Agreements: A Practical Guide to Personal Freedom.* San Rafael, CA: Amber-Allen Publishing, 2001.

"Student Reports of Bullying: Results from the 2017 School Crime Supple-ment to the National Crime Victimization Survey." National Center for Education Statistics, July 2019. https://nces.ed.gov/pubs2019/2019054.pdf [PDF].

Vogels, Emily A., Risa Gelles-Watnick, and Navid Massarat. "Teens, Social Media and Technology 2022." Pew Research Center, August 10, 2022. https://www.pewresearch.org/internet/2022/08/10/teens-social-media-and-technology-2022/.

"Warning Signs of Mental Illness." American Psychiatric Association. Accessed December 3, 2022. https://www.psychiatry.org/patients-fami

lies/warning-signs-of-mental-illness.

Wiseman, Teresa. "Concept Analysis of Empathy." *Journal of Advanced Nursing* 23, no. 6 (1996):1162–1167. https://doi.org/10.1046/j.1365-2648.1996. 12213.x.

About the Author

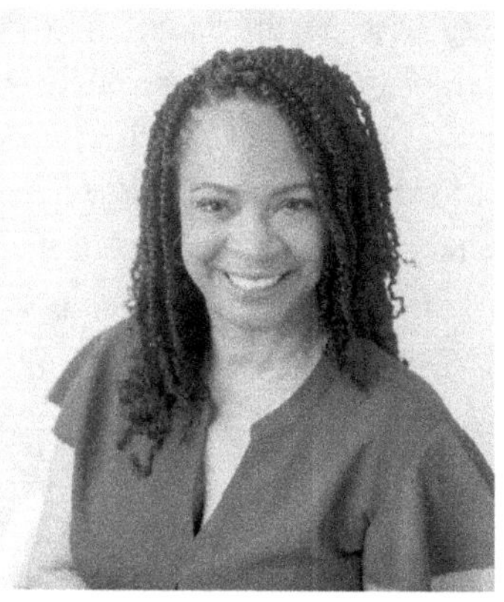

Dr. Alaina Johnson is a clinical psychologist and mother of three creatively driven boys.

When she took a temporary break from her practice to relocate with her son while he performed on Broadway, Dr. Alaina connected with parents of other creatively driven teens and tweens. She quickly recognized universal themes in the parenting questions and challenges these parents navigated as they worked to best understand, support, and affirm their children and their children's passion.

To facilitate her own parenting journey and better respond to the requests for guidance she was receiving from other parents, Dr. Alaina began searching for resources specific to parenting teens and tweens drawn to the creative arts. She discovered that there were very few parenting resources that addressed the unique needs and challenges of adolescent creative artists.

Upon her return to her clinical practice, Dr. Alaina began building Parenting Talent to provide guidance to address this need. With Parenting Talent, she works as a consultant, instructor, writer, and speaker specializing in supporting parents, families, teachers, and coaches of creatively driven teens and tweens.

Dr. Alaina lives with her husband and three sons outside of Chicago. She enjoys taking walks in nature, exploring new places, and eating great meals with close friends. She considers herself fortunate that she is truly enjoying the turn her career has taken... since her retirement funds have largely gone to her boys' instruments, music lessons, and acting classes.

A Gift for You

Whether you're a parent or another amazing grown-up who cares about talented, creative, artistic teens and tweens, thank you for choosing this book to help you gain some insight and understanding in your quest to best support them.

I know from the fact that you've read this book that doing whatever you can to support the creative teen or tween in your life is one of your most important priorities.

If we want to be able to offer our best guidance and support to others, though, we have to make our own self-care a top priority. Overlooking or neglecting our own self-care not only impacts our own well-being, but it also inhibits our ability to take care of others. We can do all of the reading, listening to podcasts, and engaging in parenting classes in the world, but we won't be able to properly implement what we've learned if we have not attended to our own needs.

To show my appreciation for your commitment to supporting the creatively driven teen or tween in your life, I want to offer my support to you in your self-care implementation or expansion journey. To receive your free gift, sign up at www.parentingtalent.com/self-care-journey.

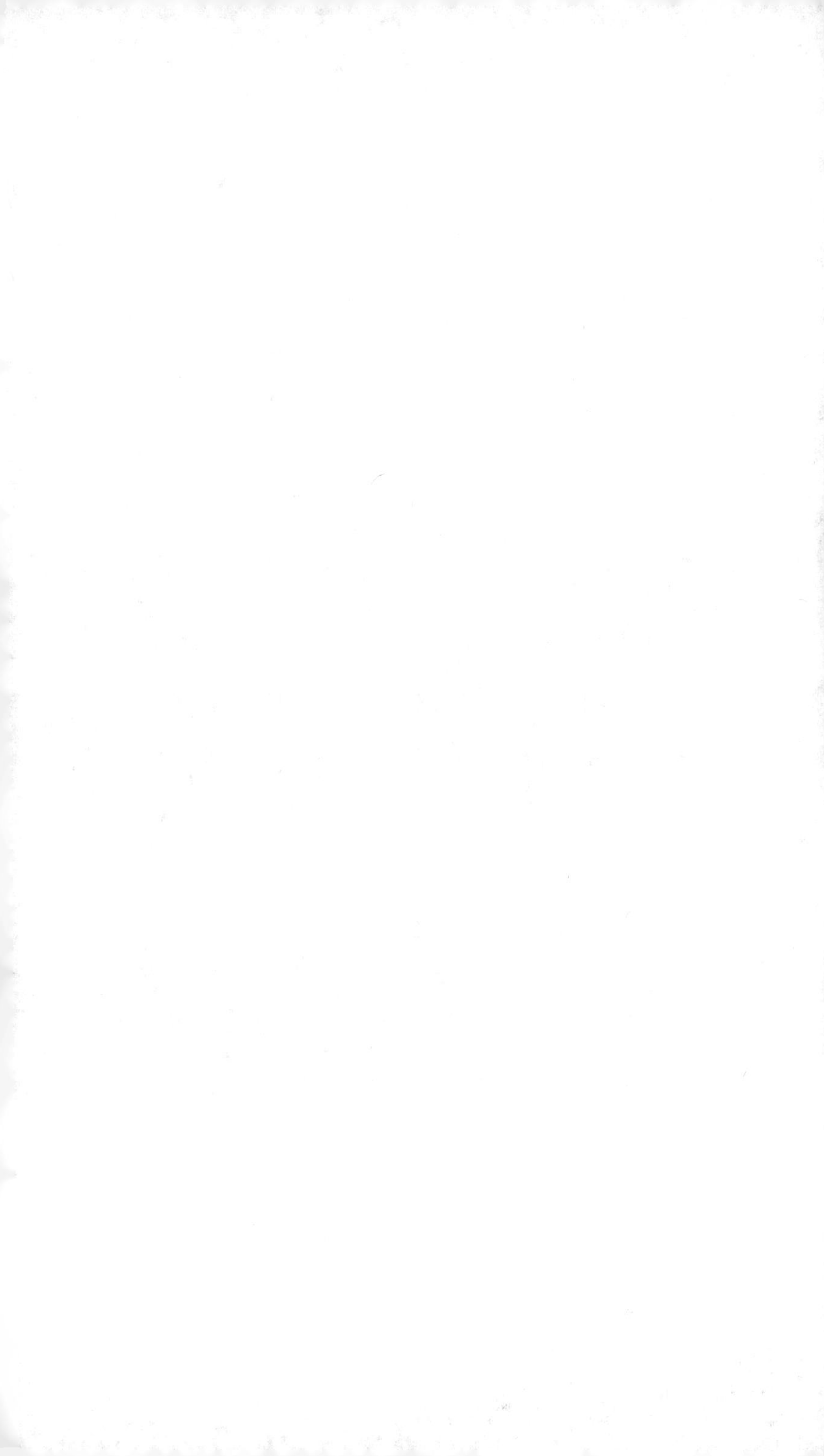